AIRLI

SAAB 340

MICHAEL MAGNUSSON

SAAB-FAIRCHILD 340

SWEDAIR REGIONAL AIRLINER

COMAIR

CS

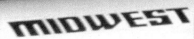

am

Disclaimer

The author has taken every effort possible to ensure that the information published is correct at the time of writing. However, many sources, including other publications, have been consulted and the author can not be held responsible for erroneous information published elsewhere or given in good faith consequently the author can not be held responsible for any subsequent use made of the published information.

As always when writing a book, one is dependent on the help and advice of many individuals and companies. First of all I would like to thank Mike Savage of Saab Aircraft International. Without his support this book would not have been possible. I would also like to thank Ron Sherman of Saab Aircraft of America who has proof-read and checked the entries of the US operators. The staff of the Saab marketing teams in England, Sweden, Hong Kong and USA have also been a great help. Norman Pealing was very helpful in letting me go through his archives and get the necessary transparencies prepared.

Other that have contributed with information and/or pictures are: Eddy Gual (Aviation Photography of Miami), Bill Gould (Philip Morris), Antonio Härry (Crossair), Tommy Lakmaker, Dick Phillips, Select Air Productions (Australia), Reimar Wendt, Earl Wilson (Kelly Springfield).

The following sources have been used: *Air Transport World*, *Airfinance Journal*, *Aviation Week*, *Aviation Letter*, *CRAN & CRANI*, *Commuter Air*, *JP Airline-Fleets International*, *Professional Pilot*, plus annual reports and press-releases from Saab-Scania and various operators.

Although Michael Magnusson is employed by Saab, this book has been produced in his spare time, and consequently Saab will not accept responsibility for any part of this book.

Overleaf: The classic picture of the first four Saab 340s in formation over the countryside near Linköping, Sweden. Picture was taken in March 1984. *(Saab-Scania, Å. Anderson)*

Copyright © Michael Magnusson

First published in the UK in 1991 by
Airlife Publishing Ltd.

British Library Cataloguing in Publication Data
A catalogue record of this book is available from the British Library

ISBN 1 85310 269 5

Printed by Kyodo Printing Co (S'pore) Pte Ltd, Singapore

Airlife Publishing Ltd.

101 Longden Road, Shrewsbury, SY3 9EB, England.

Introduction

Privately owned Saab Aircraft in Sweden is probably best known for its military aircraft which have been trend-setters for many years. Aircraft like the 'Flying Barrel', the 'Draken' and the 'Viggen' have put the Saab name at the forefront of military aircraft technology. Lately Saab has established itself firmly in the regional aircraft market with its Saab 340.

This all began in 1979. During that year Saab initiated studies for a new 30-seat regional aircraft together with Fairchild, based outside New York. This resulted in a co-operation agreement being signed on January 25 1980. In this agreement, Fairchild would manufacture the wing and tailplane at its Republic factory on Long Island, and Saab would manufacture the fuselage and be responsible for final assembly at its new plant in Linköping, Sweden. Initial project name was '3000' but in July 1980, it was officially named 'Saab-Fairchild SF-340'. About the same time General Electric was selected as the engine supplier with its new CT-7 engine derived from the T-700 helicopter unit. Meanwhile Saab had placed a group of engineers with Fairchild to design the aircraft. Most of 1980 went to define the aircraft and build a wooden mock-up in Linköping.

Marketing of the aircraft began immediately and early customers were Crossair in Switzerland, Swedair in Sweden and Comair and Air Midwest in USA. In late 1981 production began in the brand new facilities in Linköping adjacent to the military factory. By early 1982 major sub-assemblies were finished and the first wing was lifted out of the jig in April. The fuselage and wing were mated in August. The great moment of actually rolling out the prototype came on October 27 in the presence of the Swedish King. This was quickly followed by the first flight on January 25 1983. After a hectic flight test period lasting some 16 months involving four aircraft, the SF-340 (as it was then called) received its type-certificate on May 30 1984. First 340 for a customer was delivered on June 6 when Crossair received its first aircraft. This was placed into service on June 15 flying from Basle to Paris. On June 29 the JAR certificate was awarded. The 340 was the first aircraft to be certified under the new JAR rules in which Belgium, Finland, France, Germany, Holland, Norway, Sweden, Switzerland and the UK participated. The American FAR certificate was awarded at the same time. Australia followed on October 30.

By January 1985 Swedair and Comair had also introduced the 340 on their respective networks.

However, Fairchild soon entered economic problems. Partly due to the increased costs of starting up the 340 programme and partly because of the T-46 programme. When the USAF finally cancelled the T-46, Fairchild decided to withdraw from the aircraft business altogether. Swearingen in Texas was sold and an agreement was reached with Saab to withdraw from the 340 programme. Consequently as of November 1 1985, Saab took over the complete responsibility for the 340 and renamed it the 'Saab SF-340'. In 1987 it became simply the 'Saab 340' and the factory in Linköping was expanded to take over the wing- and tail-production.

After that the pace increased. The 100th 340 was delivered in September 1987 and at the same time the improved 'Saab 340B' was launched. It had more powerful engines, higher cruise speed and could carry more payload. From aircraft number 160, all 340s are 'B' models.

The number of aircraft sold has increased steadily. In 1987 and 1988 44 340s were sold each year. In 1989 Saab sold 123 aircraft, of which 50 were to AMR, the parent-company of American Airlines. the 300 mark was reached in 1990, and at the time of writing, the number stands at 334 with over 250 delivered.

TABLE OF COMPARISONS		
	340A	**340B**
First flight date:	January 25 1983	April 21 1989
Accommodation:	30–37	30–37
Wing span:	21.44 m (70 ft 4 in)	21.44 m (70 ft 4 in)
Wing area:	41.81 sq.m (450 sq.ft)	41.81 sq.m (450 sq.ft)
Length:	19.7 m (64 ft 9 in)	19.7 m (64 ft 9 in)
Height:	6.87 m (22 ft 6 in)	6.87 m (22 ft 6 in)
Max. t/o weight:	28,000 lb	28,500 lb
Max. land. weight:	27,200 lb	28,000 lb
Max. payload:	8,085 lb	8,285 lb
OEW:	17,615 lb	17,715 lb
Typical cruis. speed:	275 kt	285 kt
Range:	805 nm (35 pax)	980 nm (35 pax)
T/o field length: (MTOW, ISA, SL)	3,900 ft	4,050 ft
Max. ceiling:	25,000 ft*	25,000 ft
	2000	
First flight date:	Early 1992	
Accommodation:	50–58	
Wing span:	24.76 m (81 ft 3 in)	
Wing area:	55.7 sq.m (600 sq.ft)	
Length:	27.03 m (88 ft 7 in)	
Height:	7.73 m (25 ft 4 in)	
Max. t/o weight:	48,500 lb	
Max. land. weight:	47,400 lb	
Max. payload:	13,000 lb	
OEW:	29,770 lb	
Typical cruis. speed:	360 kt	
Range:	1,000 plus nm (50 pax)	
T/o field length: (MTOW, ISA, SL)	less than 4,920 ft	
Max. ceiling:	31,000 ft	

(* executive version 31,000 ft)

AER LINGUS COMMUTER (EI)   Ireland

Aer Lingus was founded as the national airline of Ireland in 1936. Based in Dublin, it operates a fleet of about 30 aircraft including B-747s and B-737s of all models. Aer Lingus formed a commuter division in 1984 to handle regional routes and its first aircraft was a Shorts 330 delivered during the spring of 1983 for the routes from Dublin to Liverpool and Leeds/Bradford. However, the aircraft soon became too small, and an order for four SD-360s was placed. With the 360s, Aer Lingus Commuter introduced new services to Bristol, Cork, East Midlands, Edinburgh and Shannon. More capacity was needed on some routes and consequently an order was placed for four Fokker 50s (later increased to six). By now the network had grown to include Glasgow, Guernsey, Newcastle, Cork, Galway and Sligo. Services were also operated from Cork to Birmingham, Bristol, Brussels, Manchester and Rennes.

In order to offer an improved services on its existing routes, Aer Lingus Commuter started evaluating pressurized 30 seat aircraft.

The Saab 340B was selected, and an order for four aircraft was signed in January 1991 for delivery the same year. These four 340Bs, configured with 34 seats, will replace the SD-360s in the fleet.

Chief Executive is Ray Wilson, and Aer Lingus Commuter has 220 employees. In 1990 it flew 423, 550 passengers. Domestic routes being planned for the 340Bs are from Dublin to Galway, Sligo, Kerry, Derry and Knock. International routes planned are Leeds–Bradford, East Midlands and Newcastle.

Saab 340B Fleet

EI-CFA	248	Jun.91/	'St. Eithne'
EI-CFB	251	Jun.91/	'St. Aoife'
EI-CFC	255	Aug.91/	'St. Finbarr'
EI-CFD	257	Aug.91/	'St. Senan'

A pre-delivery shot of Aer Lingus' first Saab 340 *(Saab)*

AIGLE AZUR (ZI)   France

The present day Aigle Azur was founded in 1970 as Lucas Air Transport. Based at Pontoise airfield outside Paris, it operated mainly light aircraft during the 1970s on ad-hoc charter work. In September 1980 it purchased a secondhand Bandeirante. This was followed during the 1980s by various Beech King Airs.

By 1990 it had added two Falcon 20s and changed its name to Aigle Azur.

In late 1989 it purchased a single Saab 340A from the then bankrupt Air Limousin. This aircraft has mainly been used for ad-hoc charter work and as a backup aircraft for Crossair. During spring 1990, Aigle Azur negotiated with **Industrie Air Charter** (IAC) regarding a potential lease of the aircraft. IAC was then planning to begin flying the Carcassonne–Paris route starting May 1990 and the intention was to buy its own 340B but pending delivery it would lease the Aigle Azur aircraft. However, it soon postponed the start-up until September, and eventually ceased operations completely in November.

The present Aigle Azur fleet is one Saab 340, two Falcon 20, one Bandeirante, three Beech King Airs and a single Beech Queen Air. Its managing director is Jean Denis and it has about 25 employees.

It should perhaps be mentioned that during the 1950s there was another Aigle Azur. This airline had started operations in September 1946 with Junkers 52s, and later added DC-3s and C-46s. It flew in the Mediterranean area, but also set up separate operations in Vietnam and various places in Africa. The airline was taken over by UAT in 1955.

Saab 340A Fleet
F-GGBV   086   Nov.89/

The Aigle Azur 340 in Basle (A. Härry)

AIR BREMEN (HR)   Germany

Air Bremen was the brainchild of Gus Boots, who saw a need for direct air services to Bremen. He had earlier been KLM's sales manager for northern Germany and, after KLM withdrew from the Amsterdam–Bremen route, he saw the possibility of setting up a regional airline in Bremen. Consequently the company was organized early 1988 after three year's evaluation. The Saab 340A was chosen after the company had evaluated both the ATR42 and E-120. Final contract for two 340As was signed on September 16 1988. By then the shareholders had been signed up, comprising Salenia in Sweden with 25 per cent, Bremen City 35 per cent and the remainder spread amongst prominent Bremen corporations including Securitas and Cargo Levant & Sloman Neptun.

Gus Boots took delivery of the first 340 in Linköping on February 17 1989, and with this aircraft initiated scheduled services on March 28, from Bremen to Copenhagen. This route was flown twice daily, along with a twice daily route to Brussels. With the delivery of the second 340 on March 31, Air Bremen began flying from Paderborn via Munster to London-Stansted. Paderborn was dropped after a few weeks so that the route went Bremen–Munster–London.

A third 340A was leased from Salenia in October 1989, and with the expansion of the fleet Air Bremen began flying to Vienna.

Likewise it began flying in co-operation with **Air France** on the Bremen–Paris (CDG) route.

In early 1990 it signed a co-operation agreement with **American Airlines**. This agreement called for a third daily rotation to Brussels using the 'AA' code. Likewise it began flying to Amsterdam in co-operation with **KLM**, from March 1990. Unfortunately the airline kept losing money with average passenger-loads less than predicted. Air Bremen had simply tried to develop too many new routes unsupported. As the owners were not willing to contribute more money, the airline was forced to cease operations on August 22 1990 and declare bankruptcy. Talks were held with KLM regarding taking a stake in the airline but this was not concluded. Unsuccessful attempts were also made by Interflug to take over the airline.

Saab 340A Fleet

D-CHBA	141	Feb.89/Aug.90	'Paula Modersohn B.'
D-CHBB	144	Mar.89/Aug.90	'Georg Duckwitz'
D-CHBC	159	Oct.89/Aug.90	'Wilhelm Kaisen'

An Air Bremen 340A on a pre-delivery test-flight *(Saab)*

AIR LIMOUSIN T.A. (ALTA) (QD)   France

Air Limousin began operations in January 1979, based at Limoges. Initial fleet was light aircraft plus a single Twin Otter. It soon added a single Beech 99 and two Nord 262s. By 1985 the fleet had grown to four Nord 262s, plus the Twin Otter. The Beech 99 was sold late 1984 in Sweden.

Business activities initially consisted of scheduled air-services from Limoges to Brive, Perigueux and Bergerac, plus aerial photography and aircraft sales. Later, routes were added to Lyon, Marseille and Nantes. General Manager was Joel Blais. By 1988 it had some 190 employees.

In 1986 ALTA was awarded **Air France** routes from Toulouse and as these routes were enough to keep one aircraft busy it decided to buy two Saab 340s. One was for the Air France operations and the other for existing scheduled routes. This in order to start replacing the Nord 262s. A contract was signed with Saab for two aircraft on December 17 1986 and the 340 intended for their own routes was guaranteed by the local Chamber of Commerce.

Both 340s were delivered during spring 1987, one sporting the full Air France livery and the other Air Limousin's own colours. The 'Air France' 340 was based in Toulouse and flew on behalf of Air France to Frankfurt, Brussels and Amsterdam. The other was based in Limoges and flew the routes to Brive and Lyon. During summer months it also flew from Limoges to Nice, and from Nice to Deauville.

During 1988, Air Limousin was hard hit by air traffic control problems in France and high pilot turnovers. This, plus other problems, produced large losses and by December 1988, Air Limousin had accumulated a 42 million Franc deficit. Consequently on December 30 it was placed under administration pending a reorganization. Operations did continue and during spring 1987, Dirac SA of Marseille negotiated to buy the airline. When these attempts failed, the airline ceased operations on April 28 1989. Two days later it was officially liquidated.

TAT bought the Air Limousin fleet for resale, including the two 340s. The Air France operation out of Toulouse was taken over by Brit air, using their own 340 aircraft.

The general manager, M. Blais later moved to Basle were he set up a new regional airline, namely Alsavia, also with Saab 340 aircraft.

Saab 340 Fleet

F-GGBJ	085	May87/Apr.89	Sold Kendell
F-GGBV	086	Apr.87/Apr.89	Sold Aigle Azur

The only 340A that was painted in their own livery
(E. Gual/Aviation Photography of Miami)

AIR MIDWEST (ZV/AMW)   USA

Air Midwest was founded in 1965 by Gary M. Adamson in Wichita as Aviation Services Inc (ASI). The first equipment was a Cessna 206 which was used to carry corpses. However, it soon branched off into aerial ambulance work.

The opportunity to enter the scheduled air service market presented itself in 1967 when another airline withdrew from the Wichita-Salina market. Gary Adamson stepped in with two round trips per day. Three months later he added Wichita-Springfield service. However the economics were bad and the airline almost went out of business when the US Post Office stepped in; ASI got mail-contracts for seven routes. Two more Ce.206s and a Ce.402 was added. This was followed by a Beech 99 in 1968. The following year it changed name to Air Midwest. The network expanded steadily and the first of many Metros arrived in 1976. Small profits were achieved in 1974, 1977, 1978 and 1980. In 1982 it made a $1.9 million profit. In the same year 309,000 passengers were carried with 22 Metros. By 1985 this had doubled to 761,000 passengers but the company made a loss of $3.6 million. In 1986 Air Midwest carried 921,848 passengers.

As traffic grew in the 1970s, Air Midwest started evaluating bigger equipment. On August 30 1980 it signed an order for three Saab 340As. Another two were ordered on February 13 1981. Air Midwest became the first US operator to order the 340. The first was officially presented at a ceremony at Wichita on March 27 1985. It entered service on April 1 linking Wichita with Kansas City, as well as Manhattan and Omaha. The second 340 entered service on April 15 opening up routes to Springfield, Kansas City and Dallas. Later Des Moines was added to the 340 network. All maintenance was done at the Springfield base. The final three aircraft arrived later the same year. As Air Midwest was a FAR Part 135 operator, the 340s were operated with a 30 seat layout.

At the end of 1984, Air Midwest announced the acquisition of Scheduled Skyways, based in Fayetteville, Arkansas. By mid-1985 Scheduled Skyways had been completely integrated with Air Midwest. The combined fleet consisted of 40 Metros and five Saab 340s with 800 employees. Scheduled Skyways had ordered ten E-120s. Four were delivered but another six sold before delivery to ASA.

In May 1985 Air Midwest agreed to start using the EA designator for its flights out of Kansas City from November 1, thus linking up with **Eastern**'s hub. Two months later it joined up with **Ozark** in St Louis. On January 28 1986, it announced a feeder agreement with American whereby it would operate out of Nashville as an **American Eagle** carrier. However, it retained its own network out of

Wichita. The 340s mostly flew out of Kansas City to Wichita while the E-120s flew out of Nashville. When Ozark was taken over by TWA, the St Louis operation became a **TW Express** feeder in December 1986.

Operations expanded, in 1987 Air Midwest passed one million passengers, and two more 340s were added to the fleet. In January 1988 Robert Priddy became the new president and CEO. Founder Gary Adamson remained as chairman. In September 1987 Air Midwest sold its Eagle operation in Nashville to AMR for $8 million. This deal included 11 Metros. The E-120s were moved to the St Louis hub. At this time Air Midwest was passing through some economic difficulties. The problems increased when Eastern departed from Kansas City, and Air Midwest terminated the feeder agreement on September 14 1988. As Braniff moved in to replace Eastern, Air Midwest signed a new feeder agreement with Braniff the following day. For Braniff, Air Midwest flew its 340s to Lincoln, Omaha, Des Moines, Cedar Rapids, Madison, Little Rock, Fayette-ville and Manhattan.

Early in 1989 Air Midwest ordered 15 Jetstream 31s to start replacing the Metros. During 1989 Air Midwest carried 912,000 passengers.

New problems arose when Braniff went bankrupt in September 1989. Air Midwest continued to fly out of Kansas City but traffic obviously dropped drastically. It shifted some 340s to its St Louis

operation but it was obvious that the fleet was too large. Consequently four 340s was disposed during February and March 1990. However by now the airline was in serious financial difficulties. Its St Louis operation was sold to Resort, the other TW Express carrier in St Louis. The remaining part of Air Midwest finally accepted a take-over offer from Mesa and merged with this airline early 1991. At the same time the last 340s were phased out. During 1990 Air Midwest boarded 797,455 passengers, a reduction of 12.6 per cent from the previous year.

Saab 340A Fleet

N342AM	011	Feb.85/Mar.90	'Bernice', sold PLM
N343AM	019	Mar.85/Mar.90	'Kansas City Spirit', sold PLM
N344AM	030	Sep.85/Mar.91	To Express A/l
N346AM	032	Oct.85/Mar.91	To Express A/l
N347AM	039	Nov.85/Mar.91	'Ray Ryan', to Express A/l
N935MA	073	Jul.87/Feb.90	'Milt Adamson', to Express A/l
N922MA	077	Aug.87/Feb.90	To Express A/l

Photograph on previous page shows Air Midwest's basic livery as used on most aircraft *(Author)*

After becoming a Braniff partner, Air Midwest started repainting its 340s in their new livery, but only one (N346AM) was repainted prior to Braniff's closure. Picture above shows N346AM taxying at Kansas City *(Author)*

AIR NELSON (PG)   New Zealand

New Zealand has seen a dramatic change of its air transport system in the past few years. Traditionally, New Zealand's air-traffic has been handled by two state-owned airlines, namely Air New Zealand for all international routes and New Zealand National Airways Corporation for all domestic operations. These two were joined in 1978 as Air New Zealand. Ten years later the airline was privatised. At the same time, the government opened up the market so that Ansett was allowed to set up a local airline and compete with Air New Zealand. This airline now operates a fleet of BAe.146s and DHC-8s.

To control the traffic and remain competitive, both airlines have associated regional airlines. In **Air New Zealand**'s case, it has purchased 50 per cent of Eagle Air and Air Nelson. Some regional routes are also flown by the subsidiary Mount Cook Airlines with BAe.748s as well.

Ansett has formed alliances with five other smaller airlines who operate under the 'tranzair' names.

Air New Zealand has for many years flown the Fokker F27 on its smaller routes. In order to become more cost-effective, it decided to close down these operations and Air Nelson stepped in to take up the slack.

Air Nelson, with its base in the city of the same name, was founded in 1976. Initial business was mainly ad-hoc charter and flying school activities. When Air Albatross ceased operations, it moved into scheduled services. Initially flying Piper Navajos, it then started upgrading to Metro IIIs. The Metro fleet had expanded to nine aircraft by 1990 when the last three joined the fleet.

When taking over part of the F-27 operation from Air NZ, a bigger aicrcraft was needed. The choice was the Saab 340, and in order to start operations quickly, four 340As were leased during last quarter of 1990. At the same time they took up options on four new 340Bs.

The first two 340As were placed into service on November 13 1990 between Wellington to Nelson and Blenheim. With more aircraft added, 340 operations started to New Plymouth, Tauranga, Taupo, and Auckland. As one 340 was returned to LAPA, it was replaced by another plus a second for expansion making a fleet of five aircraft. Current managing director is Robert M. Inglis.

Saab 340A Fleet

ZK-FXA	120	Oct.90/	Leased from Crossair
ZK-FXB	122	Sep.90/	Leased from Crossair
ZK-FXC	069	Nov.90/Apr.91	Leased from LAPA
ZK-FXD	088	Nov.90/	Leased from Crossair
ZK-NSL	141	Apr.91/	Leased from Saab
ZK-NSM	144	May 91/	Leased from Saab

Air Nelson's 340A sporting a modified Crossair livery *(Saab)*.
However, the last two 340s have been repainted in the new 'Air NZ Link' livery.

AIR VENDÊE (VM)

France

Another French regional airline that has chosen the Saab 340, Air Vendee is based in La Roche-Sur-Yon and started operations in 1975 but scheduled services did not begin until 1979. Initial fleet consisted of light aircraft and a single BN Islander. The fleet was fairly stable until mid 1980s when four King Air 100s was added. Then followed a rapid expansion with Twin Otter, Metro and Dornier 228 equipment joining the fleet. In 1990 the fleet consisted of seven Metro/Merlin IV, two Dornier 228s, one King Air and one Piper PA-42.

The network had by this time grown considerable and international routes were now operated from Nantes to London (Gatwick), Brussels, Barcelona and Amsterdam along with domestic services from Nantes to Rouen, Le Havre, and from Rouen to Lyon. Latest addition to the network is Nantes–Geneva, inaugurated in April 1990. Along with the expanding network, the traffic is increasing. In 1989 it carried 48,000 passengers and in 1990 61,000. Its two main operational bases are Nantes and Rouen. However, there are some services with Metros from La Roche.

During 1989 it started evaluating new 30-seat aircraft and after a tight race between Embraer and Saab, the latter got the order. On August 22 1989, Air Vendee signed for three 340Bs with a 36-seat QC interiors. Deliveries were for spring 1991, autumn 1991 and spring 1992. The 340s would initially replace the two leased 228s in the fleet, but would also eventually replace the Metros.

Main base for the 340s is Rouen, where a new runway has been built. The first 340 was delivered in March and ferried to Rouen. On April 2 1991 it entered service on the Rouen–Lyon and Rouen–London (Gatwick) routes. Later on, the 340s will be introduced on the Nantes–Geneva sector, which was inaugurated in April 1990, and from Nantes to Brussels. However, final route-definition will depend on the traffic growth.

The airline is owned and chaired by Jean-Paul Dubreuil. The general manager is Nicolas Japy.

Saab 340B Fleet

F-GHVS	230	Mar.91/
F-GHVT	276	Nov.91/
F-		92/

Pre-delivery shot of Air Vendee's first 340B *(Saab, N-G. Widh)*

ALPHALINES/AIR EXEL (DN)   Switerland/Belgium

Alphalines is the management company of the Esquel Group. Its President and major shareholder is Charles Bemberg. The company runs a number of regional airlines in various European countries and is in the process of setting up more.

First came Air Exel in France which was founded in 1988, based in Lyon. Its fleet consists of three E-120s, some operated on their own routes and others leased out. This was followed by Air Exel (UK), based at Luton, also with E-120s. So far these have been leased out as they have not yet succeeded in starting their own scheduled services.

In December 1988, Alphalines ordered two 340Bs, intended for onward lease to Italy. Four months later they signed for another two. As a consequence of the Italian operation not going ahead, Alphalines cancelled two 340Bs at the end of 1989 and leased the other two to Südavia in Munich. When this airline ceased operations, the aircraft were transferred to the newly created Air Exel Belgium.

This airline had been set up in 1989, based at Liege. Its shareholders are Luxembourg-based Esquel holdings 40 per cent, Charles Bemberg 34 per cent and TEA 26 per cent. However, their start-up was delayed by the drawn out procedure of allowing regional airlines to operate international routes from regional airports in Belgium. Up to now this had been Sabena's monopoly. Air Exel (Belgium) thus started operating the Liege–Paris route on June 11, 1990, on behalf of Air Exel (France). This was soon followed by Liege–Nice service. Another route planned is Liege–Lyon as soon as permits can be obtained. Early 1991 Air Exel (Belgium) began operating the routes under its own name and consequently re-registered the aircraft in Belgium. For the summer season of 1991, Air Exel Belgium planned to fly to Nice, Charleroi, Lourdes and Biarritz.

Long-term plans are to introduce routes to England and Germany using the two 340Bs, which have a unique 35 seat quick change interior. This gives Air Exel the possibility to fly them on both passenger and cargo services.

Saab 340B Fleet

OO-RXL	163	Dec.89/
OO-RXM	171	Dec.89/

Air Exel's 340B *(Saab, N-G. Widh)*

ALSAVIA (AF)   France

Alsavia was organized in late 1988 as a French regional airline to be based at Basle (Mulhouse) Airport. Initially the owners were going to be just Crossair and Air France, but after long negotiations, TAT joined as a partner. The shares were split as follows: **Air France** 14 per cent, **Crossair** 33 per cent, TAT 19 per cent, the remainder held by Alsatian business interests. Initial capital was FFr 50 million.

First aircraft was a 340B delivered directly from Saab in November 1989. This aircraft was part of the Crossair 340B order, and the aircraft was maintained by them.

Operations began on December 4, with routes from Basle (Mulhouse) to Amsterdam, Milan and Barcelona. As all these routes are flown on behalf of Air France, the 340 is painted in full Air France livery. In May 1990 a new service was launched from Strasbourg to Dusseldorf, this following the termination of the Milan route.

Current plans calls for some TAT Brasilias to be added to the fleet. These will fly services on behalf of TAT.

The single 340B was returned to Crossair in April 1991. Current plans are to lease other 340s in the future.

General Manager is Joel Blais, formerly of Air Limousin.

Saab 340B Fleet
F-GKLA   168   Nov.89/Apr.91

Alsavia's single 340B in Air France livery *(A. Härry)*

AMR (AA/AAL) USA

AMR Corporation, the holding company of American Airlines, is today one of the major players on the world airline scene. Most statistics on this so called 'mega-carrier' are impressive. Its current fleet consists of some 500 jet aircraft with over 200 more on order. In 1989 American carried 72 million passengers, coming second only after Aeroflot. It has about 75,000 employees. Most importantly of all, it is one of the most profitable airlines operating today, with some $445 million in profit in 1989.

American early recognised the importance of establishing feeder airlines at its major hubs. In 1984 AMR established its feeder operation under the name of 'American Eagle'. It tied up various independant airlines such as Command in New England, Metro in Texas, Air Midwest in Nashville, and Simmons in Chicago. In order to secure more firmly the ties with the major airline, AMR later started buying up these feeder carriers.

First came Nashville. AMR bought the Nashville operation of Air Midwest together with 11 Metros in September 1987. Then followed in quick succession during 1988 Command (with ATR-42s and SD-330/36s), Simmons (SD360s and ATR-42s), Executive Air in San Juan (C-212s and ATR-42s), AV Air in Raleigh-Durham (Metros) and finally Wings West in San Luis Obispo (Metros). Two American Eagle airlines remain independant for the moment, these are Metro in Dallas and Chaparral Airlines in Abilene, Texas. (These two merged in 1990 under the 'Metroflight' name). By now there were more than 200 aircraft within the Eagle operation servicing 142 cities out of seven hubs.

AMR then embarked on an ambitious re-equipment drive. For the 19-seat requirement it ordered 25 Jetstream 31s plus 25 options. For the 30-seat requirement it chose, after a long evaluation, the Saab 340B. On May 24 1989 AMR signed a contract for 50 Saab 340s with 50 options. It was the biggest in the regional aviation history. Delivery rates would be 15 in 1990, 24 in 1991 and 11 in 1992. This delivery schedule was later accelerated. AMR later ordered 16 ATR-42s and nine ATR-72s to fill the gap for 40+seat aircraft. Some 340 aircraft are expected to be in service within the American Eagle system by 1995.

At a special ceremony in Linköping in January 1990. AMR's Chairman and President Robert Crandall accepted the first Saab 340B. It entered service on March 15 on the Nashville–Indianapolis route. The AMR 340s are equipped with 34 seats and are the first 340s with Hamilton-Standard propellers and TCAS.

The first batch of 340s was delivered to the Nashville operation. This division has its origin in the Air Midwest operation which started in April 1986. It was purchased by AMR at the end of 1987. The network was expanded during 1988 when 17 new cities were added and a new hub was set up at Raleigh-Durham after AMR took over AVAir. During 1989 another 13 cities were added and a new hub set up in Miami after Eastern began having problems. During this year the Nashville Eagle carried 645,511 passengers. The Saab 340s were initially based in Nashville but soon aircraft were operating in both Miami and Raleigh-Durham.

By the end of that year, 18 340Bs were in service and their success prompted AMR to announce a firm order for 20 more 340Bs and 20 options in January 1991 for delivery during 1993. The total AMR order thus is 70 340B on firm order and 50 options. The Nashville Eagle operation was by now handling 90 Saab 340 flights per day.

Early 1991, AMR announced the merger of Command Airways and Nashville Eagle. The new operation, named 'Flagship Air Lines', will operate out of four hubs (Nashville, Raleigh-Durham, Miami and New York) and serve 87 destinations by the end of the year. By then the fleet will consist of 45 Jetstream 31s, 34 Saab 340Bs, 13 ATR42s, and 12 SD-360s. The Metros will be transferred to Wings West in California.

During 1990 Nashville Eagle carried 1,103,897 passengers, an incredible 71 per cent increase from 1989. On the other hand Command reduced its boardings to 510,951.

During spring 1991 the first 340s were delivered to Wings West.

Heavy maintenance of the Saab 340Bs is contracted out to FFV Aerotech in Nashville. Training has been done at Flight Safety in San Antonio, but AMR will soon receive its own Saab 340B simulator which will be installed at AMR's training centre in Dallas.

Saab 340B Fleet

Reg	Serial	Date	Note
N174AE	174	Jan.90/	
N177AE	177	Mar.90/	
N180AE	180	Mar.90/	
N184AE	184	Apr.90/	
N191AE	191	May 90/	
N193AE	193	Jun.90/	
N194AE	194	Jun.90/	
N198AE	198	Jul.90/	
N201AE	201	Aug.90/	
N202KD	202	Aug.90/	
N203NE	203	Sep.90/	
N204NE	204	Sep.90/	
N210AE	210	Oct.90/	
N211NE	211	Oct.90/	
N214DA	214	Nov.90/	
N218AE	218	Nov.90/	
N219AE	219	Dec.90/	
N222NE	222	Dec.90	
N227AE	227	Feb.91/	
N231LN	231	Mar.91/	Wings W
N232AE	232	Apr.91/	
N234AE	234	Mar.91/	Wings W
N235AE	235	Mar.91/	
N236AE	236	May 91/	
N238AE	238	May 91/	
N240DS	240	May 91/	
N241AE	241	May 91/	
N243AE	243	May 91/	
N244AE	244	Jun.91/	
N245AE	245	Jun.91/	
N247AE	247	Jun.91/	
N250AE	250	Aug.91/	
N253AE	253	Aug.91/	
N254AE	254	Aug.91/	
N256AE	256	Sep.91/	
N259AE	259	Sep.91/	
N261AE	261	Oct.91/	
N263AE	263	Oct.91/	
N264AE	264	Oct.91/	
N266AE	266	Nov.91/	
N268AE	268	Nov.91/	
N269AE	269	Nov.91/	
N272AE	272	Dec.91/	
N273AE	273	Dec.91/	

Another 26 on order for 1992/3

Photograph shows AMR's first Saab 340B prior to delivery *(Saab)*

AVIATION ASSOCIATES (EA)   USA

This airline started off as Sunaire in 1982. Its base was St Croix in the US Virgin Islands. The first aircraft were a PA-31 Navajo and a single DHC-6 Twin Otter. Flying between the US Virgin Islands and Puerto Rico, its fleet of Twin Otters grew rapidly. In 1985 the airline was purchased by **Metro** in Dallas, and it entered an agreement with Eastern to become the feeder at San Juan. By 1986 its fleet had grown to ten Twin Otters, all sporting Eastern's colours and flying as **Eastern Metro Express**. Eastern had established a hub in San Juan on November 1 1986. In 1987 it changed its formal name to Aviation Associates Inc. Its executive VP was then Robert Philips and it had 153 employees. Destinations served from San Juan were Aquadilla, Mayaguez, St Croix, St Maarteen, St Thomas, Tortola and Virgin Gorda.

Late 1986 it signed an agreement with Saab to lease two Saab 340As. Both aircraft were delivered in mid-January 1987 and stayed for three months. Technically the operation was a success, however with the high frequency short-haul nature of the airline, the 30 seat pressurised aircraft did not fit so both aircraft were returned. This however paved the way for a large order from Metro in Dallas (see under 'Metro').

Aviation Associates went back to its Twin Otters, and were flying 11 of these aircraft on behalf of Eastern up until Eastern's bankruptcy in January 1991. After Eastern's closure, Aviation Associates began using its own ticket stock and its own code 'OY' from January 15. In February Metro Chairman E. A. Henderson and President Jay Seaborn bought the operation from Metro for $6.5 million. The airline reverted to its old name 'Sunaire'. Now with 12 Twin Otters it continued to serve six Caribbean cities including San Juan, St Croix and St Thomas. Passenger boardings for 1990 were 429,224.

Saab 340A Fleet

| N922MA | 077 | Jan.87/Mar.87 | Leased from Saab |
| N935MA | 073 | Jan.87/Mar.87 | Leased from Saab |

Photograph depicts Aviation Associates Saab 340 in Eastern Metro livery
(Select Air Productions)

BANGKOK AIRWAYS (BKP)   Thailand

Bangkok Airways was set up in 1986 by Dr Prasert. Its main business was to have carried tourists to Samui Island. An order for two Saab 340As was announced at the Farnborough Air Show in September 1986. However, construction of the new airfield at Samui Island was delayed and Bangkok Airways was unable to take delivery of the aircraft which were resold to other customers.

A new attempt to relaunch the airline was successful and Bangkok Airways decided to lease two DHC-8s from GPA as they were readily available. These were delivered in April and September 1989. However one year later, on November 21, one of the DHC-8s crashed on approach to Samui Island with the loss of 38 lives. It was replaced by another DHC-8 from GPA, this time a DHC-8-300.

Saab 340A Fleet

HS-SKH	068	Never delivered, resold
HS-SKI	—	

The only 340A that was painted in partial Bangkok Airways livery *(Author)*

BAR HARBOR AIRLINES (EA)   USA

Bar Harbor was founded in 1946 by Thomas and Joseph Caruso as a seaplane charter, air taxi and sight-seeing operator. Initial equipment was a Piper Cub.

In 1968 Bar Harbor began scheduled passenger service between Bar Harbor and Bangor, Maine. Equipment was Cessna 310, this was followed by Cessna 402s the following year. In 1970 a non-stop Bar Harbor–Boston service was added. More route additions followed in 1972, these being Portland, Maine and Quebec City. At the same time it introduced Beech 99s. Presque Isle became the sixth destination in 1973. The rest of the 1970s saw a continued steady expansion of the fleet and the network. However, it was marred by a tragic aircraft accident in 1978 when co-founder Thomas Caruso, General Manager Gary Caruso and two more were killed. Joseph and Allyn Caruso assumed control of the airline.

In 1980 Manchester, Worcester, Rockland, Waterville and La Guardia in New York were added to the network. At this time its fleet consisted of three Convair 600s, 10 Beech 99s, two Cessna 402s, once Cessna 310 and a Cessna 206. The following year it carried its millionth passenger and signed a marketing agreement with Eastern. This meant that Bar Harbor's flights were listed in Eastern reservation system and that it shared gate and terminal space at some airports.

In 1982 New York John F. Kennedy was added to the network. The subsequent year Bar Harbor ordered ten Beech 1900s which started arriving in 1984. Philadelphia was added to the network. This was followed by Burlington and Newark in 1985.

The original Eastern agreement was redone in 1986 so that Bar Harbor started operating as an **Eastern Express** carrier with the 'EA' designation. Bar Harbor would mainly feed Eastern's hub in Boston. It also agreed to start up an operation in Florida on behalf of Eastern. First route was Miami to Key West. The initial fleet in Florida consisted of four Beech 1900s. By now its total fleet had grown to six Convair 600s, ten Beech 1900s, eleven Beech 99s, seven Cessna 402s and a Cessna 310. Number of employees stood at 350 and it carried 357,719 passengers in 1985

On March 1 1986 Bar Harbor purchased Valley Airlines in Maine. To start replacing the Convair 600s, Bar Harbor ordered four Saab 340As in September 1985 with two options. The two options were converted to firm orders the following year. The first four arrived during the summer of 1986 and were assigned the operation in New England. Initial 340 service was flown on June 18 from Bangor via Boston and Albury to Portland. As Bar Harbor was an Eastern Express carrier, all the 340s were painted in full Eastern Express livery. Maintenance was done at its Bangor base.

In April 1987, Texas Air bought 50 per cent of Bar Harbor. Another 35 per cent was purchased through an Eastern subsidiary. As a consequence of this PBA, already being a subsidiary of Texas Air, was merged with Bar Harbor under the Bar Harbor name. Allyn Caruso stayed as president (later replaced by Thomas Barbour). Bar Harbor now started flying as a **Continental Express** carrier as well as an Eastern Express feeder. The merger process was completed by September 1988. As Continental had a hub at Newark, Bar Harbor set up a large operation at this airport including the 340s, which were repainted in the Continental livery during 1989. It still operated sizeable operations in Boston and Miami for Eastern.

More changes followed in 1990. In July, Eastern Airlines bought part of Bar Harbor from Continental in order to operate it purely as a Florida division. The New England operation of Bar Harbor was retained by Continental. With the purchase went the six 340s as well as six Beech 99s and ten Beech 1900s. The Miami hub was then flying 47 services per day to 11 destinations in Florida and the Bahamas. Jack Robinson was appointed as new president. However the changes did not end here. Early 1991 Jack Robinson together with a group of investors attempted to acquire Bar Harbor from Eastern. However, on January 18 1991, Eastern ceased operations.

As a consequence of this, Bar Harbor ceased flying and filed for bankruptcy two days later. All aircraft were grounded in Miami. The negotiations between Robinson and the bankruptcy court continued, meanwhile all the Saab 340s were repossessed and leased to Express Airlines. Currently all Beech 99s and 1900s remain and no agreement has yet been reached between Robinson and the bankruptcy court.

Saab 340A Fleet

N401BH	057	Jun.86/Jan.91
N402BH	058	Jun.86/Jan.91
N403BH	060	Jul.86/Jan.91
N404BH	061	Jul.86/Jan.91
N406BH	074	Nov.86/Jan.91
N407BH	078	Dec.86/Jan.91

Previous page, the Bar Harbor 340s were initially painted in the Eastern colour-scheme. In this photograph, one of the 340s is flying over Miami *(Saab/N. Pealing)*

Above, after purchase by Continental, five of the 340s were repainted in Continental Express livery *(Author collection)*

After the return to Eastern, these were once again painted in a modified Eastern livery

BIRMINGHAM EUROPEAN AIRWAYS (VB)

Great Britain

Birmingham Executive Airways, as it original name read, was registered as a private company on March 1 1983. Orders were soon placed for Jetstream 31s, of which the first two were delivered in May the same year. These aircraft were fitted with a 12 seat executive interior. On June 8 BEA operated its first service, from its base at Birmingham Airport, to Zurich, and to Copenhagen on the following day. A third route to Milan was delayed for six months due to difficulties in obtaining necessary approvals. All these routes were flown daily, and another two routes, Glasgow and Aberdeen, were flown on behalf of British Airways. As traffic grew, BEA started evaluating larger aircraft, and eventually selected the Saab 340. An order for one was placed in September 1984, and this aircraft was delivered in February the following year. On March 8 it entered service on the routes to Copenhagen, Glasgow, Zurich, Geneva and Milan. This 340 had a unique 27 seat executive interior.

Unfortunately BEA soon experienced a larger than average share of early teething problems with the aircraft. Some of these problems were connected with BEA's long-distance high-altitude routes. Saab introduced various modifications to solve the problems. After BEA's 340 operations, this aircraft saw service with Manx and later NetherLines.

After a degree of reorganization of its management in 1986, BEA purchased three secondhand Gulfstream G-1s to complement its Jetstreams.

The Pilmsoll Line acquired the airline in November 1988 and major shareholders are British Airways and Maersk, each having a 40 per cent holding.

In 1990 the new management decided to introduce jet aircraft, and acquired five BAC-111-400s. They currently operate to Amsterdam, Copenhagen, Frankfurt, Milan, Oslo, Newcastle and Stuttgart. Planned additions to the network are Stockholm and Gothenburg. By now the airline has changed its name to Birmingham European Airways.

Saab 340A Fleet

G-BSFI	008	Feb.85/Dec.85	'Spirit of Scandinavia'

BEA's single 340A at Metair in West Malling *(Saab)*

BRIT AIR (DB)

France

Brit air was founded as an air taxi company by its present president, Xavier Leclercq, in 1973. The following year it acquired its first two aircraft, Piper Aztecs, which were followed two years later by a Piper Cheyenne. Based at Morlaix, in the north-western part of France, it soon found a growing list of clients as the region was poorly served by scheduled airlines. In 1977 the local Chamber of Commerce purchased the majority of the shares.

In 1979 Brit air launched its first scheduled services, to London (Gatwick). This was soon followed by Quimper, and from Rennes to Caen, Le Havre and London. For this purpose it bought two new Bandeirante aircraft. In 1981 routes were opened between Rennes to Lyon. By this time the Bandeirante fleet had grown to four and Brit air carried 32,400 passengers in that year. The following year the company signed an agreement with Air Inter. On behalf of this airline it began flying from Quimper and Rennes to Paris and for this purpose acquired two Fokker F-27s. Passenger boardings jumped spectacularily to 150,000 in 1983. The company also inaugurated a modern office and hangar at its base in Morlaix. The following year it introduced a new service from Caen via Le Havre to Lyon.

The year 1986 marks another important milestone in Brit air's history. In that year it signed an agreement with **Air France** to start operating regional services on their behalf. At the same time it introduced its first two new ATR-42s. These Air France routes are from Paris and Lyon to various international destinations such as Bristol, Bremen, Dusseldorf, Stuttgart, Zurich, Milan and Vienna. Passenger boardings took another jump to 232,000 in that year, and continued to increase steadily to 286,000 in 1987 and 320,000 in 1988.

With an expanding network, Brit air soon saw a need for an aircraft between the 19-seat Bandeirantes and the 46–50 seat F-27/ATR-42s. Evaluations began for a suitable aircraft, and Brit air soon settled for the Saab 340. An order for one aircraft was placed in December 1986 and the aircraft was delivered in March the following year. On April 1 it flew Brit air's first 340 service. This

aircraft was soon followed by more new 340As from the manufacturer plus a second-hand one from EAS, making a fleet of six 340s by 1989. With these additions to the fleet, passenger boardings jumped again to 435,500 in 1989. Of these 28 per cent were on Brit air's own routes, 42 per cent on their Air France routes and 30 per cent on Air Inter services.

By 1990 Brit air had become the third biggest regional airline in France with a fleet of six ATR-42s, six Saab 340s, three Bandeirantes, two King Airs and one Piper Cheyenne. The last two types used for air taxi work. The F-27s have been sold and future types currently being evaluated or planned are ATR-72s (four have been ordered), Saab 2000 (four options held) and Embraer/CBA 123 (five options).

Of the six 340s, three are painted in Brit air's own colours. These fly during weekdays Rennes–Le Havre–London (Gatwick) twice daily and on weekends the same route, but via Caen. Other routes include Brest–Toulouse.

The remaining 340s are painted in full Air France livery and on behalf of this airline they currently operate from Paris to Eindhoven, London (Stansted), Southampton and Cardiff and from Nantes to Dusseldorf and Milan. When Air Limousin went bankrupt, Brit air took over their 340 routes flown on behalf of Air France from Toulouse. Currently these are Barcelona, Nice and Frankfurt. The Air France destinations changes regularly depending on demand.

Saab 340A Fleet

F-GELG	081	Feb.89/	Ex EAS
F-GFBZ*	083	Mar.87/	
F-GHDB	117	Apr.88/	
F-GHMI	153	Jun.89/	
F-GHMJ*	136	Dec.88/	
F-GHMK*	143	Mar.89/	
SE-ISC	008	Nov.88/Dec.88	Leased from Saab

(* Brit air livery)

One of Brit air's 340s flying over its Morlaix base *(Saab/C. Skelding)*

BROCKWAY (METRO AIRLINES NORTHEAST) (TW)

USA

Brockway has been flying the New England skies for the past 20 years, albeit under different names and liveries.

The origins of Brockway are Air North and Clinton Aero Services. Air North began in the late 1960s as a Mohawk Airlines feeder to five cities in upstate New York. When Mohawk was absorbed by Allegheny, Air North became an Allegheny Commuter. At this time it was operating Twin Otters to Watertown, Ogdensburg, Massena, Plattsburg and Saranac. After the deregulation of 1978, Allegheny terminated its relationship with Air North, who continued as an independent carrier. With new SD-330s and F-27s, Air North expanded its network. President of Air North at this time was John Sullivan.

Clinton Aero Services was founded in 1972 by Anthony Von Elbe and James Drolette as a charter and FBO operation. Clinton initially flew a shuttle service between Plattsburg and Burlington with a Piper Aztec and a Cessna 402. Later it took over some routes from Air North, and added Beech 99s and later Beech 1900s.

Brockway Inc was founded 1907, and has since grown to one of the world's largest manufacturer of glass and plastics. By late 1980s it employed 13,000 people. Having already purchased Crown Airways, Brockway went ahead and purchased Air North and

Clinton Aero in the summer and autumn of 1983. J. Sullivan became president of the joint operation, although all three airlines continued as separate operations. Crown continued as a US Air feeder in Pittsburgh with SD-330s. The other two dropped their original names and became Brockway Airlines, although the old Air North continued as a FAR Part 121 operation with Fokker F-27s, and Clinton as a FAR Part 135 operation with Beech 1900s. After successful negotiations Brockway became a **Piedmont** feeder during the spring of 1986. Crown Airways continued as a US Air feeder.

To start replacing the Fokker F-27s, Brockway began evaluating new aircraft. It finally chose the Saab 340 and ordered five plus five options on March 24, 1987. The first 340s, sporting the Piedmont livery, entered service during the summer. By the end of 1987, all five 340s were in service. Its fleet then consisted of the five Saabs and 11 Beech 1900s. Main base was and still is Burlington in Vermont. Brockway fed into the hubs in Boston, New York, Philadelphia and Washington. In 1986 it carried 717,516 passengers.

Happy with the first five 340s, Brockway converted its five options to firm order in August 1988. In October it signed a new ten-year agreement with Piedmont connecting at its hub in Syracuse. At this time they served 23 cities in five north eastern states.

Meanwhile, the holding company, Brockway Inc, had been purchased by another large glass-manufacturer, Owens-Illinois. Owens subsequently decided to sell part of its airline operation. After lengthy negotiations during the spring of 1989, Metro of Dallas purchased Brockway (both the New York based and Vermont based, but not Crown Airways) for $14.2 million on April 7. It was renamed **Metro Airlines Northeast**. Along with the sale went five Saab 340s and 11 Beech 1900s. At the same time Metro Northeast signed a ten-year code-sharing agreement with TWA, effective from July 1 1989. New president was ex Metro VP Planning, Doug Caldwell. John Sullivan and Tony Von Elbe left. During 1988, the two Brockway operations had carried 570,000 passengers. The aircraft were quickly repainted in the **TW Express** livery and the remaining 340s joined the fleet during the same year.

Faced with reducing (586,151 passengers) traffic and increased costs in 1990, Metro decided to transfer two 340s to its Dallas operation in December. Number of employees was cut back from 520 to 449. The beginning of 1991 saw further traffic reductions. At the same time Metro was facing large losses at its Atlanta operation after Eastern's closure on January 18. Consequently, Metro decided to close down its operation in the northeast. On February 7, Metro Northeast ceased all operations cancelling service to 23 cities.

At the time of writing, ZAL Holdings Inc was negotiating to purchase the operation from Metro for $3.9 million. It is still unclear what aircraft would go with the new operation, but all 340's had been placed with Business Express.

Saab 340A Fleet

N741BA	090	May 87/Feb.91	'Spirit of Vermont'. To Business Express
N742BA	092	Jun.87/Feb.91	'Spirit of New York' To Business Express
N743BA	093	Jun.87/Feb.91	To Business Express
N744BA	105	Oct.87/Feb.91	To Business Express
N745BA	111	Dec.87/Feb.91	To Business Express
N746BA	138	Dec.88/Feb.91	To Business Express
N747BA	148	May 89/Feb.91	To Business Express
N748BA	149	May 89/Feb.91	To Business Express
N749BA	152	Jun.89/Feb.91	To Business Express
N751BA	157	Sep.89/Feb.91	To Business Express
N752BA	091	Jan.90/Nov.90	Leased from Metroflight
N753BA	089	Jan.90/Nov.90	Leased from Metroflight

Note: First five delivered in Piedmont livery. N746BA delivered all white. Remaining delivered in basic or full TW Express colours.

Photograph on previous page shows initial Piedmont livery *(Saab/N. Pealing)*
The final TW Express colours as seen above on this 340 taxying in Burlington *(Author)*

BUSINESS AIR (GNT)   United Kingdom

This small Scottish airline was founded in 1987 by Ian Woodley. Based at Aberdeen, it started operations with a Piper Navajo, a Cessna 404 and three Bandeirantes. All aircraft were leased. Based on the experience of Euroair, they began scheduled services. These grew rapidly and hence they introduced a Shorts 360 leased from JEA in October 1988. Its main routes were then Dundee–Manchester and Esbjerg.

However, Business Air needed an aircraft with increased payload, primarily for its Royal Mail contracts, and thus started evaluating pressurized 30-seaters. A Salair 340 was demonstrated to them on January 20 1990 at Edinburgh. Impressed by its qualities, Business Air decided to incorporate such an aircraft in its fleet. Meanwhile **Crossair** had taken an interest in the growing airline, and soon a deal was struck. In August 1990 Crossair acquired 15 per cent of Business Air and provided a 340. Ian Woodley maintained a 70 per cent share of the company, and the balancing 15 per cent is owned by the Abela Corporation. Initially they leased an ordinary

340 while Crossair converted another to 'Quick Change' configuration. This aircraft was delivered in April 1991. However, once this 340 was delivered, Business Air decided to keep the other as well.

The 340 flies the Aberdeen–Dundee and Manchester as well as Esbjerg routes on behalf of several oil-companies. On September 24 it began flying mail at night from Aberdeen via Edinburgh and Newcastle to Luton. This currently is the airline's main business.

On October 29 it started flying on behalf of **British Airways**, operating a morning service between Aberdeen and Birmingham, and late afternoon service from Birmingham to Edinburgh replacing BEA's G-1.

Saab 340A Fleet

HB-AHL	082	Sep.90/	Leased from LX (To be reg. G-GNTB)
G-GNTA	049	Apr.91/	Leased from LX ('QC')

Business Air's newly delivered Saab 340 G-GNTA *(Saab)*

BUSINESS EXPRESS (DL)   USA

Business Express is a rapidly expanding Delta feeder in New England. Like many successful airlines it had humble beginnings. The origin of Business Express is Atlantic Air. This airline was founded in 1982 in Bridgeport, and began flying to Boston and Philadelphia. Its fleet consisted of Piper Navajos. However it soon entered financial difficulties. Consequently in November 1984 it was purchased by Marketing Corporation of America (MCA). President and CEO of MCA is James R. McManus. MCA also owns a Saab car dealership, realty firm, restaurant chain and software company. McManus had been frustrated with the lack of air-service to the Bridgeport area, and now saw an opportunity to develop. Atlantic Air was relaunched as Business Express. The network was expanded to include Baltimore, Martha's Vineyard, Nantucket and White Plains. Operational and administrative headquarters were moved from Westport to Hartfords Bradley International Airport. The five Navajos were replaced by five Beech 99s. In the subsequent 18 months, Business Express added 16 Beech 1900s to replace the Beech 99s. Passenger boardings increased six-fold the following 12 months. More destinations were added like New Haven and Groton.

In March 1986 Business Express purchased Pilgrim Airlines. Its six Fokker F-27s were incorporated in the Business Express fleet while its single F-28 and eight Twin Otters were disposed of. This added 11 new destinations in the northeast plus three in Canada. Business Express was by now the largest regional airline in the northeast.

In June 1986 it joined the **Delta Connection** programme replacing Ransome which had been bought by Pan Am. From then on it fed Delta's hubs in Boston and New York (La Guardia). During this year it carried 525,000 passengers.

To start replacing the F-27s, Business Express ordered six Saab 340s plus four options in August 1986. These entered service the following year. Business Express also leased four Shorts 360s. With more aircraft, the traffic increased. In 1987 it carried 651,000 passengers. In the same year it completed its new maintenance base at Bradley Airport. MCA continued to be headquartered in Westport.

During 1988 the F-27s were gradually phased out. The network had by now grown to 24 cities, with Boston being the largest hub followed by New York (La Guardia). Otherwise 1988 was a year of consolidation for Business Express which had expanded very rapidly.

However, early 1989 saw another large aircraft order, in March Business Express announced its decision to incorporate another nine Saab 340s (one 340A and eight 340Bs). This was followed with another order for 18 Saab 340Bs in November. At the same time ten options were signed for the new Saab 2000. Business Express has thus ordered 33 Saab 340s and become one of the major operators in the world. The additional 340s will replace the SD-360s as well as some Beech 1900s.

In August 1989 Business Express purchased Mall Airways in Albany, New York. Its two Beech 1900s were incorporated into the fleet but their seven Beech 99s returned to the lessors. Total boardings for 1989 were 936,000. After the demise of Metro Northeast, Business Express leased their ten 340A's.

Business Express current fleet is 18 Beech 1900, 13 SD-360, 17 Saab 340A, and eight Saab 340B (18 more on order for 1991–93).

Business Express (DL) — continued

Number of employees is 650. It serves 25 cities in the northeast with 450 daily departures including Toronto and Montreal in Canada.

During 1990 it carried 1,126,059 passengers, a 16 per cent increase over 1989.

Saab 340A Fleet

N340BE	062	Oct.86/	
N341BE	063	Oct.86/	
N342BE	096	Aug.87/	
N343BE	101	Sep.87/	
N344BE	104	Oct.87/	
N345BE	108	Dec.87/	
N346BE	150	Jun.89/	
N741BA	090	May 91/	Leased
N742BA	092	May 91/	Leased
N743BA	093	May 91/	Leased
N744BA	105	May 91/	Leased
N745BA	111	May 91/	Leased
N746BA	138	Apr.91/	Leased
N747BA	148	May 91/	Leased
N748BA	149	May 91/	Leased
N749BA	152	May 91/	Leased
N751BA	157	May 91/	Leased

Saab 340B Fleet

N347BE	187	Apr.90/
N348BE	190	May 90/
N349BE	196	Jun.90/
N350BE	197	Jun.90/
N351BE	237	May 91/
N352BE	239	May 91/
N353BE	242	May 91/
N354BE	246	Jun.91/

18 more on order

Previous page, Business Express carries its own livery as a Delta feeder, as shown on this 340 taxying in Burlington *(Author)*

However, early 1991 it introduced a revised colour-scheme, above *(Saab)*

CHAUTAUQUA AIRLINES (US)   USA

Chautauqua Airlines was set up in 1974 to replace Allegheny Airlines on the routes from Jamestown to Pittsburgh and Buffalo. The founder of the airline is Joel Hall. Joel Hall started his career as a pilot with Mohawk Airlines in 1962. He flew Convairs, FH-227s and BAC-111s. In 1967 he became chief pilot. When Mohawk was bought by Allegheny in 1972 he stayed on for a while. With the fuel crisis of 1973, Allegheny started cutting back weak routes, including the Convair 580 service from Pittsburgh via Jamestown to Buffalo. Hall decided to set up a regional airline in Jamestown to fill the gap. He promptly ordered a pair of Beech 99s and began operations in 1974. A third Beech 99 arrived in August 1977. Considering Hall's background with Mohawk and Allegheny, it is not surprising the airline has from day one been an **Allegheny Commuter**.

With more routes and increased traffic, Chautauqua acquired two Shorts 330s in 1979. Hall continued a steady expansion and by 1985 five Metro IIIs had joined the fleet. Number of employees was 185. The following year it carried 358,000 passengers.

To replace the unpressurized SD-330s, Chautauqua ordered two Saab 340As in December 1987. These two entered service in October 1988. As Chautauqua is a FAR Part 135 operator, the 340s have 30 seats.

By now Chautauqua had seven Metro IIIs, the two 340As and the three Beech 99s. One Beech 99 was based in Florida to fly between Orlando and Vero Beach. Chautauqua had a large semi-circular network from USAir's hub in Pittsburgh. Destinations included Hamilton in Canada, Hagerstown, Roanoke, Youngstown and Akron. The two 340As mainly fly from Pittsburgh to Jamestown, Roanoke and Akron.

Although the feeder arrangement remained fairly intact, things were changing with the partner. Allegheny changed name to USAir in October 1979, but kept its commuter system under the old name of Allegheny Commuter. US Air subsequently purchased PSA in May 1987 and Piedmont in November. The merger with Piedmont was not completed until August 1989. To reflect the identity of the new airline, the commuter system was renamed **USAir Express** as of July 1 1989. With the new name went a new livery which was progressively introduced on the aircraft. The 340As of Chautauqua were repainted towards the end of 1990.

USAir had also purchased a number of its feeder airlines such as Pennsylvania Airlines in 1985 and Suburban in 1986. Piedmont had purchased Henson in the same year. However Chautauqua remained independent although the ownership changed in 1988 when Transmark, a Florida insurance company, purchased the airline. Tom Hall (no relation to Joel Hall), formerly with Transmark is currently president and CEO. In December 1989, Chautauqua ordered four Saab 340Bs for delivery in 1991. Number of passenger boardings in 1989 had grown to 441,000, and 479,078 during 1990.

In the autumn of 1990, Chautauqua decided to terminate its Florida operation. Effective from January 1991, it ceased flying to Gainsville, Tampa, Vero Beach and Orlando. The three Beech 99s stationed in Florida were put up for sale.

Saab 340A Fleet

N125CH	125	Sep.88/
N128CH	128	Oct.88/

Saab 340B Fleet

N224RH	224	Jan.91/
N233CH	233	Apr.91/
N252CH	252	Aug.91/
N274CH	274	92/

Below, the first two 340s were painted in the Allegheny Commuter livery *(Saab)*
Overleaf, after USAir Express was launched they were repainted in the new USAir Express colours *(Saab/N. Pealing)*

CHICAGO AIR (ML)   USA

Chicago Air was founded in the autumn of 1985 to fly regional air-services out of downtown Midway Airport in Chicago. In March it announced an order for ten Saab 340s plus six options. Deliveries were to start in October the same year. In order to start operations during the summer, Chicago Air leased six Fokker F-27s from Midstate. The first service was flown on May 29.

However, passenger load-factors did not meet expectations and the start-up airline began losing money heavily. After Chicago Air defaulted on some lease payments, Midstate took over the airline in October. Four of the six F-27s were replaced with Metros. The founder Neal Meehan left the airline (later joining Continental Express). Bryce Appleton of Midstate replaced him as president. Nearly 100 employees were furloughed. Amongst the destinations served were Wausau/Stevens Point, Eau Claire, La Crosse, Madison, Green Bay, Peoria, Springfield and Traverse City.

Deliveries of the Saab 340s were delayed and later cancelled. The first two 340s were actually painted in full Chicago Air colours but resold prior to delivery.

Midstate continued the operations with a few Metros for a few more months before ceasing operations. Midway Airlines later established its own feeder airline at Midway Airport by purchasing Fischer Brothers Aviation and renaming it Midway Express. It today operates a large fleet of Dornier 228s.

Saab 340A Fleet
N340CL	069	Never delivered
N341CL	072	Never delivered
N342CL to N350CL reserved		

One of the two 340s that were painted in full Chicago Air colours *(Saab)*

COMAIR (DL)

USA

Comair owes its existance to the deregulation of the United States domestic passenger regulations in 1978. Prior to this, Raymond Mueller noticed how unprofitable routes were being dropped by the major airlines. Together with his son David, he founded Comair in 1977 to exploit such routes. Using two Piper Navajos, he began flying from Cincinnati to Cleveland and Akron (Canton) in April 1977. By 1980 the fleet had grown to five Navajos and two Chieftains (nine seat version of Navajo). By now the Navajos were too small on some routes, consequently Comair started adding Bandeirantes to its fleet. The first two were ordered in 1981.

The number of passengers increased rapidly. In 1979 Comair carried 33,814 passengers, the following year 50,683, and then 78,370 in 1981. During 1982 the number of passengers almost doubled to 138,946. During the same period, the number of employees went from 35 to 245. In 1982 the fleet consisted of nine Bandeirantes, seven Chieftains, and four Navajos.

Based on the growth trends of the airline, Comair ordered four Saab 340As on October 2nd 1981. Although Air Midwest had ordered the 340 in 1980, Comair became the first US airline to put it into service. With the continued strong passenger growth, Comair ordered another eight 340s on November 9 1983.

To meet a short term need for more capacity, Comair leased five Shorts 330s for different periods between 1981 and 1987. However, as soon as the 340 fleet was built up, the 330s were returned to the lessors.

To replace the Bandeirantes, Comair purchased five Metro IIIs in 1983. Just prior to the introduction of the 340s, the Comair fleet consisted of ten Bandeirantes, five Metro IIIs, and five SD-330s. In 1983 it carried 234,662 passengers and employed 326 persons. The number of destinations had grown to 14. Starting in the north these were Detroit, Cleveland, Toledo, Columbus, Indianapolis, Dayton, Charleston, Huntington, Nashville, Evansville and Lexington. Louisville and Birmingham were added in April 1983. Comair also inaugurated a new $2 million operations and maintenance facility at the Greater Cincinnati International Airport.

The first 340 was handed over the Comair on July 30 1984. It was then used for training flights until placed into service on October 1. Before the end of the year another two 340s had joined the fleet. The remaining nine arrived during 1985 and Comair had chosen a 33 seat layout for their 340s.

In the same period, on September 1, Comair became a **Delta Connection** carrier and started using Delta's flight-numbers. Later, in July 1986, Delta purchased 20 per cent of Comair's stock.

Happy with the 340s in service, Comair signed an order for another three on May 8 1985 (for delivery in 1986). This was followed by a final order for three in 1988, making a total of 18 340s. Another aircraft was leased.

With the arrival of the 340s and the agreement with Delta, Comair entered a period of tremendous growth. In 1984 it carried 417,601 passengers and ranked 18th of the top 50 US regional airlines. By

1987 it carried 634,803 and had jumped to rank 14th. Delta developed Cincinnati into its third major hub, after Atlanta and Dallas. The number of destinations had grown to 30 including Toronto in Canada.

To handle the larger fleet — by 1987 it had grown to 12 Bandeirantes, 10 Metro IIIs, two SD-330s, and 15 340s — Comair expanded its maintenance facility in 1985 with a second hangar costing $2.5 million. Number of employees had passed 1,000, but the airline was still managed by David Mueller as president and CEO, and his father Raymond Mueller as chairman. David's sister, Gloria Weber, is manager of public and investor relations.

Comair has seen some setbacks as well. On March 10 1986, a tornado hit Cincinnati Airport and severely damaged four aircraft (including two 340s) and the newly built hangar. All aircraft and the hangar were repaired.

Next big step in Comair's expansion came in 1987 when Comair set up a new operations in Orlando, Florida. From November 1, Comair added 23 flights to seven cities being Fort Lauderdale, Daytona Beach, Melbourne, Naples, Fort Pierce, and Freeport in the Bahamas. Initial fleet was five Bandeirantes, but later all Bandeirantes were moved to Florida. Comair later ordered 40 Brasilias and took options on another 40, to replace all Bandeirantes and Metro IIIs.

Fleet in 1990 consisted of 11 Bandeirantes (Florida), 21 Metro IIIs, 14 Brasilias (another 26 on order) and 19 Saab 340s. For the future, Comair has taken options on 20 Saab 2000 and 60 EMB-145s. Passenger boardings for 1989 were 1,496,000. During 1990 the passenger boardings increased 25 per cent to 1,869,644, making it the third largest regional airline in the USA after Metro and ASA.

Saab 340A Fleet

N340CA	004	Oct.84/	
N360CA	006	Jul.84/	
N370CA	010	Dec.84/	
N380CA	012	Mar.85/	
N341CA	021	Apr.85/	
N342CA	023	Apr.85/	
N343CA	024	May 85/	
N344CA	025	May 85/	
N347CA	028	Jul.85/	
N356CA	034	Sep.85/	
N357CA	044	Dec.85/	
N358CA	047	Dec.85/	
N359CA	053	May 86/	
N361CA	056	Jul.86/	
N320CA	064	Aug.86/	
N140N	140	Mar.89/	
N146CA	146	Apr.89/	
N158CA	158	Sep.89/	
N340SF	014	Jun.88/	Leased from Amcomp. Corp.

Opposite, an early shot of a Comair 340 overflying its hometown Cincinnati *(Saab/N. Pealing)*

Above, a more recent photo of a Comair 340 taking off from Cincinnati *(Author)*

CROSSAIR (LX)

Switzerland

Crossair is very much the result of the vision of one man, its President and founder Moritz Suter. While flying as a pilot on Swissair Convair 440s and DC-9s he saw the need for a regional airline to take over some of the old CV-440 routes which could not support the DC-9.

The humble beginnings of Crossair was a company called 'Business Flyers Basel AG' founded on February 14 1975. Its first aircraft was a Piper Cub, later Cessna 320 was added. These aircraft were hired out to other pilots to fly.

Based on the experience of Air Wisconsin, and the need to fly over the Alps, Crossair selected the Metro II as its first aircraft to be used on scheduled routes. At the same time, in 1978, the name was changed to Crossair. Before the end of that year Crossair ordered four new Metro IIs from Fairchild. Although Swissair was initially very supportive of the venture, they decided not to enter as a partner. Other people stepped forward to provide the initial capital.

On July 2 1979, Crossair began scheduled operations from Zurich to Nuremberg. This together with Innsbruck and Klagenfurt were the initial routes. However, the Metro IIs proved insufficient and Crossair ordered nine Metro IIIs in 1980 with deliveries starting the subsequent year. In February 1980 Crossair had its first contact with the new Saab-Fairchild team. These discussions led to a firm order for five 340s plus five options being signed on October 2. Thus Crossair became the launch customer for the 340. When Swissair later claimed some of the Crossair routes, a severe conflict broke out. After intervention by the Swiss Transport Minister a truce was reached and a co-operation agreement signed on February 12 1982. This meant that Crossair had to give up some routes but gained others instead. Following this, Crossair converted its five 340 options to firm orders in July.

Meanwhile, passenger boardings increased rapidly. In its first full year of scheduled operations, 1980, it carried 50,000; in 1981 97,000; and in 1982 144,000. In 1984, when the 340 was introduced, 277,000 were carried.

Crossair's shares were offered to the public in 1983, and thus additional cash was raised for its continued expansion.

On June 6 1984, Crossair accepted its first 340 at ceremonies at Saab's plant in Linköping. Crossair was the first customer to receive a 340 and it also had the honour of carrying the Pope around Switzerland during his official visit. On June 15 it entered service between Basle and Paris which Crossair had taken over on behalf of **Swissair**. Its 340s were soon introduced on the routes from Basle to Amsterdam, Brussels, Düsseldorf, Frankfurt, Munich, Geneva and Zurich. In the same year, Crossair inaugurated a new maintenance hangar at Basle Airport.

The 340 fleet increased rapidly and by the end of 1985 it had grown to eight aircraft. As the 340 suffered some technical problems in the beginning of its career, Crossair being the first customer was obviously affected. However with the assistance of Saab and GE, replacement aircraft were leased in when required, while the problems were sorted out. Crossair maintained its confidence in the aircraft and ordered another three plus three options in December 1986. The three options were converted in June the following year in order to replace the remaining Metros. These were followed by another three in October and a final two in December, thus making 21 340As. Two were transferred before delivery to Delta Air, thus Crossair ended up with 19 340As. Traffic continued to increase as the fleet grew: in 1986 Crossair carried 472,158 passengers and the company continued being profitable. This figure increased to 588,328 the following year. The same year saw a renewal of the co-operation agreement with Swissair. By now it operated from Basle to Geneva and Zurich on behalf of Swissair, in addition to the Basle–Düsseldorf, Geneva–Munich and Zurich–Turin routes. Swissair has also used Crossair to launch a new route from Zurich to the Albanian capital Tirana.

Crossair tailors its service to the business passenger and consequently has installed 33 leather seats and a large double galley in the 340.

Apart from flying on behalf of Swissair, Crossair soon signed agreements with other airlines. First came **Lufthansa**, followed by **Air France** (Berne–Paris and Lugano–Paris) and **Luxair** (Zurich–Luxembourg) in 1987.

In March 1988 Crossair made a new share offer, of which Swissair took most and thus ended up with a 38 per cent stake in the airline. The airline continued to be profitable; its last loss making year was 1979. (In March 1991 Swissair increased its shares by 10.9 per cent giving a majority holding of 51.9 per cent voting rights).

When Saab announced the improved 340B version in 1988, Crossair was once again the launch customer. At the Farnborough Air Show of 1988, Crossair announced an order for five plus 15 options. In the same year Crossair flew 760,744 passenger to 26 destinations, a 29.3 per cent increase from the previous year. The year was ended with the launch of the new Saab 2000 and Crossair yet again being the launch customer, ordering 25 plus 25 options. Five of the 340B options were converted in March 1989, followed by another five in October. At the same time Crossair decided to order five Fokker 50s to bridge the gap before the Saab 2000 arrives in 1993. Crossair also decided to set up a leasing company, Aviation Financial Services, to offer some of its earlier 340s for lease. The

year finished with an order for four new BAe.146s, thus Crossair took the step up into jet aircraft. Close to a million passengers were carried (909,023) in 1990.

The beginning of the 1990s marked the heaviest investments Crossair had ever made. Apart from introducing new Fokker 50s and secondhand BAe.146s, Crossair also expanded its maintenance facility at Basle, installed a Saab 340 simulator and moved its corporate headquarters from Zurich to Basle. With a modern fleet and strong shareholders, Crossair now feels it can meet the opening of the European market in 1992.

Saab 340A Fleet

Reg	Ser	Dates	Notes
HB-AHA	005	Jun.84/Feb.90	Withdrawn
HB-AHB	007	Aug.84/	
HB-AHC	009	Oct.84/	
HB-AHD	018	Mar.85/	
HB-AHE	020	Mar.85/Mar.91	Leased Tatra Air
HB-AHF	026	Jun.85/Dec.89	Transferred Delta Air
HB-AHG	038	Nov.85/Apr.90	Transferred Delta Air
HB-AHH	040	Dec.85/Oct.90	Transferred Delta Air
HB-AHI	043	Jan.86/Sep.91	Transferred Delta Air
HB-AHK	049	Mar.86/Mar.91	Leased Business Air (QC)
HB-AHL	082	Mar.87/Sep.90	Leased Business Air
HB-AHM	084	Apr.87/	
HB-AHN	088	Apr.87/Nov.90	Leased Air Nelson
HB-AHO	113	Feb.88/	To be leased Delta Air
HB-AHP	120	Jun.88/Oct.90	Leased Air Nelson
HB-AHQ	122	Jun.88/Sep.90	Leased Air Nelson
HB-AHR	126	Aug.88/	
HB-AHS	132	Nov.88/	
HB-AHT	134	Dec.88/	
LN-NVD	037	May 88/Dec.88	Leased from Norving

Saab 340B Fleet

Reg	Ser	Dates	Notes
HB-AKA	160	Sep.89/	
HB-AKB	161	Sep.89/	
HB-AKC	164	Oct.89/	
HB-AKD	173	Dec.89/	
HB-AKE	176	Feb.90/	
HB-AKF	182	May 90/	
HB-AKG	185	Apr.90/	
HB-AKH	200	Aug.90/	
HB-AKI	208	Oct.90/	
HB-AKK	213	Nov.90/	
HB-AKL	215	Dec.90/	
HB-AKM	221	Jan.91/	
HB-AKN	225	Feb.91/	
HB-AKO	228	Mar.91/	
HB-AKP	168	Feb.91/	Ex Alsavia

Crossair introduced a new livery with the introduction of the Saab 340s.
(HB-AHK by Saab/N. Pealing)

Crossair plans to unveil a new livery during 1992

DELTA AIR (DI)

Germany

Delta Air was founded in 1978, with eight pilots and a single Twin Otter. Its base was and still is Friedrichshafen and from here it flew initially to Stuttgart and Zurich. In its first year of operations, it carried 11,310 passengers. This increased to 14,754 the subsequent year. A King Air and two Piper Cheyennes were used on air taxi work and a second Twin Otter followed in 1980. One Twin Otter was replaced by a Metro in 1982 and the other Twin Otter by another Metro in 1984. The same year, a single Dornier 228 was added. Passenger boardings had by then grown to 33,617. In 1982 the Zurich to Bremen route was added and this was followed by the Friedrichshafen–Munich and Stuttgart–Geneva routes two years later.

In 1986, ownership was restructured, so that **Crossair** took 25 per cent and Justus Dornier 70 per cent of the shares. The remaining five per cent with private investors.

With this new backing, Delta Air went ahead and ordered two new 340s in May 1986. These two aircraft were delivered at the end of the year and immediately entered service on routes to Bremen, Stuttgart, Geneva and Zurich.

The following year saw the addition of routes from Basle to Munich and Frankfurt, as well as Zurich to Stuttgart. The addition of Basle as a destination is practical in the sense that Crossair performs all heavy maintenance on the 340s. In 1988 Delta Air began operating on behalf of **Lufthansa** the Friedrichshafen–Frankfurt service. With the continued expansion of the network, Delta Air ordered another two 340s the same year. That year was ended with the introduction of a new service from Stuttgart non-stop to Barcelona as well as a Basel-Hamburg route on behalf of both Lufthansa and **Swissair**.

By this time the staff had grown to 120, and it was still being led by the founder and managing director Wolfgang Bierbach. The Metros had been phased out and the fleet was by now four 340s and a single Do-228. More than 120,000 passengers were carried. The Do-228 is used mainly for the Friedrichshafen–Munich (Oberpfaffenhofen) route.

With the fifth 340, Delta Air introduced new routes to Turin and Venice on behalf of Lufthansa and passenger boardings increased to 138,000 in 1989. The same year, Crossair increased its stake in the airline to 40 per cent. Another 59 per cent was then held by Friedrich von Bohlen und Halbach.

In late 1990, Delta Air entered former East Germany with new services from Stuttgart to Dresden and Leipzig as well as Friedrichshafen–Berlin (Tempelhof). Meanwhile more 340A's arrived making a fleet of eight by 1991, with more planned.

Saab 340A Fleet

D-CDIA	071	Nov.86/
D-CDIB	075	Dec.86/
D-CDIC	116	Mar.88/
D-CDID	124	Jul.88/
D-CDIE	026	Dec.89/
D-CDIF	038	Apr.90/
D-CDIG	040	Oct.90/
D-CDIH	043	Sep.91/
D-	113	91/

Delta Air's second 340A in its own livery *(R. Wendt)*

EUROPE AERO SERVICE (AF)　　　France

Founded in July 1965 and beginning scheduled operations one year later, Europe Aero Service (EAS) operates both charter and domestic scheduled services on behalf of Air France and Air Inter. It has mostly operated heavier aircraft such as HP Heralds, Vickers Vanguards, Caravelles and lately Boeing 727s and 737s. Major stockholder is the Masurel family. Its base is Perpignan in southern France.

With the promise of being given regional routes from **Air France**, EAS went ahead and set up a new regional sudsidiary called 'Europe Air'. They chose the Saab 340 and signed an order for one aircraft on November 21 1986. This aircraft was delivered in March the following year and became the first French 340. As it was operated on Air France routes, it was painted in full Air France livery.

Europe Air was managed by Patrice Masurel, the son of George Masurel, the president of EAS. The 340 was based at Paris (CDG) Airport and flew various Air France routes including Eindhoven, London (Stansted), Florence and Luxembourg. The aircraft was maintained at EAS' Orly base.

The venture was successful but EAS was unable to expand the regional network and consequently decided to close down its regional operation late 1988. The aircraft was leased, and subsequently sold to Brit air who took over some EAS routes.

Saab 340A Fleet

F-GELG	081	Mar.87/Feb.89

A pre-delivery shot of EAS' single 340 *(Saab)*

EXPRESS AIRLINES I INC (NW/NWA) USA

Express Airlines is the result of the initiative of one man, Michael J. Brady. Having worked for Eastern in Atlanta, he then served as president and CEO for Southeastern Airlines (now ASA), and finally started Eastern Metro Express in Atlanta, he set up his own airline marketing company in early 1985. The intention of this company, called Phoenix Airline Services, was to set up regional airlines on behalf of the major airlines. His first contract was with **Republic Express** to set up a regional operation out of Memphis. A new airline was founded, called Express Airlines I, to fulfill a ten year contract. Orders were signed with British Aerospace for 20 Jetstream 31s and with Saab for five 340s plus three options. The actual contract with Saab was signed on April 5 1985, with deliveries starting the same year. The airline operated as 'Republic Express' and all aircraft featured the full Republic livery.

With 67 employees and three Jetstream 31s, Express Airlines began operations on May 31 1985 from Memphis. Initial destinations were Monroe, La., Greenville, Miss., and Columbus/Starkville/West Point, Miss., (served by the same airport). The first 340 arrived in July, and was placed into service on July 15 to Jackson, Miss. As Express Airlines was a FAR Part 135 operator at this time, the 340 was equipped with 30 seats. Express now began a tremendous expansion; before the end of the year it had 13 Jetstream 31s and three Saab 340s in its fleet. It also signed another agreement with Republic to set up another feeder operation in Minneapolis. Operations from this hub began on December 15, 1985. Consequently more aircraft were needed. Express converted their three 340 options into a firm order in January 1986. It also ordered another ten J-31s in addition to the 20 on order. (However the last four were later cancelled).

By April 1986, Express Airlines had carried over 300,000 passengers since its start. It then had 19 J-31s and six 340s in service flying to 21 cities from Memphis and Minneapolis.

Meanwhile things were happening with partner Republic Airlines. Early 1986, Northwest made a bid for Republic Airlines, and after being accepted, the two airlines merged under the Northwest name. Consequently the Republic Express feeder network was renamed **Northwest Airlink**.

During 1986 Express Airlines carried 753,975 passengers with a fleet of 26 Jetstream 31s and eight Saab 340s. In December 1986 it ordered another three 340s making a fleet of 11 aircraft of this type.

Express Airlines continued its strong growth in 1987, with 941,841 passengers carried on the 26 Jetstreams and 11 340s. A new $3.5 million maintenance and training facility was constructed at Memphis Airport. Another smaller maintenance facility was kept in Sioux City.

During 1988 Express slowed down its growth, carrying 968,000 passengers. Nevertheless it ordered another two 340As in August. One J-31 had been lost in a ground accident in December 1987.

In 1989 Express hit a million passengers and placed a major order with Saab. In October it ordered 15 Saab 340Bs plus another ten on option. It also signed up for ten Saab 2000s. The new 340Bs will be used to replace the Jetstream 31s and for expansion.

Express Airlines employed at this time 1,000 people and operated 38 aircraft and served 40 cities in 15 states. In the same year it became a FAR part 121 operator and thus could increase the number of seats in the 340s to 33. Of the 11 340s in service in 1989, four were based in Minneapolis, the rest in Memphis. As it was short of capacity during the autumn it wet-leased three CV-580s from Sierra Pacific.

Express Airlines I Inc (NW/NWA) — continued

During the first half of 1990, Express Airlines took on seven 340As on lease in order to meet demands for still more capacity until the 340Bs start arriving. In March it unveiled the first 340 in the new bright red Northwest Airlink livery which was designed by Landor Associates in New York.

In June 1990 Express Airlines celebrated its fifth anniversary. It was now the largest privately-owned regional airline in USA carrying more than one million passengers per year. Forty destinations in 15 states are served by more than 350 daily flights. It also launched services to new destinations; from Memphis these were Columbus, GA., Shreveport, Chattanooga, and Jackson, MS. From Minneapolis it added Dubuque, IA. During 1990 Express Airlines carried 1,093,808 passengers, a nine per cent increase over 1989.

Early in 1991 Express Airlines announced that it was no longer interested in the ten CBA-123 options it had earlier taken. At the same time it appointed a UK-company to start remarketing the Jetstreams as the 340Bs started arriving. By mid 1991 it had a fleet of 31 Saab 340's.

Saab 340A Fleet

N320PX	027	Jul.85/	
N321PX	031	Sep.85/	
N322PX	041	Dec.85/	
N323PX	046	Feb.86/	
N324PX	048	Mar.86/	
N325PX	051	May 86/	
N326PX	054	May 86/	
N327PX	059	Jul.86/	
N328PX	068	Dec.86/	
N329PX	076	Dec.86/	
N340PX	079	May 87/	
N341PX	142	Apr.89/	
N342PX	147	May 89/	
SE-ISY	080	Dec.89/	Leased from Swedair
SE-F06	106	Jan.90/	Leased from Saab
N935MA	073	Feb.90/	Leased from Saab
N922MA	077	Feb.90/	Leased from Saab
SE-ISV	045	Apr.90/	Leased from Swedair
SE-KPD	037	May 90/	Leased from Salenia
SE-KPE	055	May 90/	Leased from Salenia
N401BH	057	Jun.91/	Leased ex Bar Harbor
N402BH	058	Jul.91/	Leased ex Bar Harbor
N403BH	060	May 91/	Leased ex Bar Harbor
N404BH	061	Jun.91/	Leased ex Bar Harbor
N406BH	074	Jun.91/	Leased ex Bar Harbor
N407BH	078	Apr.91/	Leased ex Bar Harbor
N344AM	030	Mar.91/	Leased ex Air Midwest
N346AM	032	Mar.91/	Leased ex Air Midwest
N347AM	039	Mar.91/	Leased ex Air Midwest

Saab 340B Fleet

N360PX	220	Feb.91/	
N361PX	249	Jun.91/	
N362PX	258	Sep.91/	
N363PX	260	Sep.91/	
N364PX	262	Sep.91/	

(Another ten Saab 340B on order for delivery 1991/92)

Express Airlines originally featured the 'Republic Express' livery as shown on previous page (D. Phillips)

When Republic was taken over by Northwest, some 340's appeared in the Northwest 'Air Link' livery, below (Saab)

Opposite, before all 340's were repainted, Northwest introduced a new all-red livery which first appeared on a 340 during spring 1990 (Saab)

FINNAVIATION (FA/AY)　　　　Finland

When Finnair introduced Fokker F-27s as a replacement to the old Convair 440s, it soon discovered that a smaller aircraft was needed to cover the thinner routes. Instead of operating such an aircraft themselves, it was decided to form a subsidiary. This was accomplished in June 1979 by merging two general aviation operators, Wihuri Oy Finnwings and Nordair, to found Finnaviation. **Finnair** supplied two thirds of the capital, and appointed Lars Dahlberg as the general manager.

Finnwings had been set up in 1950 to operate air-taxi and a flight school. Nordair was founded in 1970 as an air-taxi company. Finnaviation thus inherited a large fleet of Cessnas, Beech Barons, Aerocommanders, and Piper Cherokees. Three Bandeirantes were soon ordered and delivered within a year. Finnaviation continued the airtaxi as well as the dealership for Cessna and Gates Learjet in Finland.

On June 15, it began scheduled operations from Oulu to Luleå with a Cessna 404, which was soon replaced by Bandeirantes. The network quickly expanded to include Kuusamo, Vaasa, Kokkola, Kajaani, Kuopio, Jyväskylä and Tampere, as well as Sundsvall in Sweden.

Finnaviation held options for three Embraer Brasilias, but decided instead to order the Saab 340 as its next aircraft type. An order for three aircraft was placed in July 1985. At the same time parent-company Finnair ordered the ATR-42 to replace the Fokker F-27s. The ATR-42s were later replaced by ATR-72s, operated by the associated company Karair.

Finnaviation was the first operator to specify the 'Quick-Change' version of the 340. This enables the aircraft to be converted from a 34 passenger aircraft to a fully loaded cargo aircraft in less than an hour. This is because Finnaviation flies mail at night on behalf of the Finnish Post Office. These first three aircraft were delivered in September/October 1986 and initially placed on the services to Åbo/Turku, Tampere, Mariehamn and St Michael as well as Stockholm. Two more 340s were added in 1988, and a sixth one a year later. The last aircraft is a 'QC-VIP', as it can be converted for the Finnish government or other executive clients. With these additions, Finnaviation opened a new route from Åbo/Turku in Finland to Trollhättan (later replaced by Gothenburg). In 1988 it carried 200,000 passengers. A new hangar was also built at its base at Helsinki Airport. During the same period, Finnair increased its shareholding to 90 per cent, the remaining ten per cent held by Union Bank of Finland. By this time a new general manager had been appointed, Pekka Välimäki (later replaced by Paavo Turtiainen).

Passenger boardings increased to 240,000 the following year, and number of employees was by now 119.

In March 1990, Finnaviation began flying the Helsinki-Malmö route daily, otherwise the network has remained fairly stable. The international routes are Mariehamn–Stockholm which is flown twice daily; Turku–Copenhagen daily; Turku–Gothenburg daily and Malmö–Helsinki daily. On the domestic front, Finnaviation currently serves 17 destinations from Helsinki.

Saab 340A/B Fleet

OH-FAA	065	Sep.86/	'Norppa-Vikaren'
OH-FAB	066	Sep.86/	'Lokki-Måsen'
OH-FAC	070	Oct.86/	'Poro-Renen'
OH-FAD	135	Dec.88/	'Riekko-Snöripan'
OH-FAE	139	Dec.88/	
OH-FAF	167	Nov.89/	QC-VIP (340B)

Finnaviation introduced a new livery with the 340s *(Saab/N. Pealing)*

FORMOSA AIRLINES (HU)　　　Taiwan

Taiwan, an island of the size of the Netherlands but with 20 million inhabitants, has seen an explosion in the number of airlines since the government partially deregulated civil aviation. New airlines have sprung up and old ones resuscitated, buying new aircraft from almost every manufacturer. Consequently today one can see the Saab 340s of Formosa Airlines, DHC-8s of Great China Airlines, ATR-42s of Foshing, BAe.748s of Makung and SD-360s of China Asia all competing on the domestic scene. These in addition to the old established carriers like China Airlines and Far Eastern Air Transport. However, China Airlines is planning to give up its domestic operation and concentrate on its international routes.

Strong competition and low fares makes any operation difficult to break even. The main domestic route is Taiwan–Kaoshiung, where in early 1991 seven airlines together offer 50+ flights each way per day!

Formosa Airlines currently ranks as the third regional airline in term of passengers carried and was originally founded in 1966 as a wholly private company. It initially operated light aircraft, but in the 1970s a single DC-6B was employed on ad-hoc cargo work. The 1970s also saw the introduction of BN Islanders which continue to be an important part of the fleet. At this time the airline was known as Yung Shing Airlines.

In 1978 a group of businessmen, including Mr C. H. Hsin, acquired the majority of the shares.

The first Dornier 228 arrived in 1983, Formosa Airlines being an early customer of this type. In December 1985 the management was reorganized when Mr Hsin returned to Taiwan from USA and was elected chairman.

In 1987 the name was changed to the present Formosa Airlines. An evaluation was begun of a 30-seat aircraft and the Saab 340 was chosen. An order for two aircraft was signed during December 1987 and both aircraft were delivered the following year. A third 340 was added in 1990. Formosa selected a 37 seat layout for the 340, the first airline to do so.

Today Formosa operates the largest commuter network in Taiwan with more than 22 flights a day on 16 of Taiwan's 22 routes. Current fleet consists of three Saab 340s, six Do-228, and three BN Islanders. Number of employees is around 250. The Saab 340s are mainly used on the six daily Taipei–Kaohsiung flights, the four daily Taipei–Taitung services, but also serve Makung, Hualien, and Taichung.

In June 1991, K. H. Kao formally stepped in as the new owner and the management was changed.

Saab 340A Fleet

B-12200	127	Sep.88/
B-12266	154	Jan.90/
B-12299	129	Oct.88/

One of Formosa's 340s in Taipei (S.A.P.)

GOLDEN AIR (DC)　　　　　　　　　Sweden

Golden Air's story is really in two parts. The original Golden Air was registered in September 1976, based in Karlstad. It began air-taxi work and later night-mail with light twins. In December 1979 Golden Air began a scheduled service between Karlskoga and Stockholm using a Cessna 402. A second route was later added from Karlstad to Oslo, also connecting Karlstad with Karlskoga. The first Fairchild Metro arrived in 1982, followed by a second the subsequent year. A third was added in 1985.

The local investment company, Wermia, purchased Golden Air in 1981. Wermia is owned by prominent local business people and a local bank.

In the autumn of 1983, Golden Air took over the Örebro–Stockholm route from Swedair. This was initially subsidized by the local council but later reached breakeven.

Spring 1986 saw Golden Air began operating the Lidköping–Stockholm route. However, after two incidents with the Metros, the airline was grounded in January 1987 pending investigation. After reviewing its operating routines, the airline restarted.

Late in 1987 the airline was purchased by Gotlands-bolaget, a shipping company based at the island of Gotland, which already owned another regional airline called Syd-Aero as well as an air-taxi company called Avia. The three airlines were merged under the name Avia and its main base became Norrköping.

The general manager of the original Golden Air, Mr Göran Linden, restarted a new Golden Air based in Lidköping to operate the Lidköping–Stockholm route which was discontinued by Avia after two years of operations. Flying began with a single Fairchild Metro. In August 1989 Golden Air returned to the Lidköping–Stockholm route. At the same time a Saab 340B was ordered which was delivered in October 1989. It is equipped with 36 seats, and leased from a local bank, PK Finans AB. Its introduction into service was delayed pending Swedish BCA authorization, and it did not carry passengers until January 1 1990. Golden Air also launched services to Copenhagen connecting with Karlstad in March 1990. The airline was initially owned by Göran Linden, but ownership was changed to a group of local business people in January 1990 and the subsequent month, Åke Sveden was appointed as new general manager.

During 1990 Golden Air carried 32,000 passengers with its three Metros and single Saab 340B. The 340B is used on the six daily Stockholm flights. Number of employees is 45. Early in 1991 Golden Air was suffering financial difficulties, and shareholders were injecting more funds to correct this.

Saab 340B Fleet

SE-ISG	162	Oct.89/	'Golden Eagle'

Golden Air's single 340B in its own livery at Stockholm-Arlanda Airport, its main destination *(T. Lakmaker)*

HAZELTON AIRLINES (ZL)   Australia

Hazelton Airlines, known as the 'Big Country airline', has been flying the Australian skies since 1953. In that year it was founded by Max Hazelton to start charter services with an Auster Aiglet aircraft from his parents property at Toogong, NSW. In the beginning it was a one man, one aircraft operation but within six months a second aircraft, an Auster Autocar, was added. At the same time Max's younger brother Jim joined the growing company. In 1959 the base was moved to Cudal which remains the main headquarters today. Business grew steadily and Hazelton did everything, charter, barnstorming, carrying papers and ambulance flights, although agricultural work dominated its business. It even set a new record flying around Australia in 13 hours and 38 minutes, smashing a 31 year old record.

The 1970s saw a gradual growth of scheduled passenger services. At this time the fleet was made up of light twin aircraft such as Cessna 310s and Piper PA31 Navajos. Hazelton also had a large agriculture operation using Cessna A188s. The early 1980s saw the introduction of a pair of Beech 200 King Airs and the fleet was then over 30 aircraft. In 1983 a Bandeirante was added.

Hazelton had its greatest growth in 1988 when the network jumped from 11 to 25 destinations. This followed Ansett's take-over of East-West Airlines who were then forced by the Trade Practices Commission to give up many routes. To handle this expansion, two SD-360-300s and a Beech 1900 were purchased and put into service.

Hazelton was awarded new routes to Broken Hill, Albury, Griffith and Narrandera, since these had been taken away from Ansett NSW. Consequently, Hazelton started evaluating a pressurized 30-seat aircraft and soon selected the Saab 340B. An order for two plus two options was signed and announced at the Singapore Air Show in February 1990. At the same time two options of the Saab 2000 were taken out. Two 340As were leased as interim aircraft in order to start 340 operations quickly and the first 340A entered service on April 30 on the Sydney–Griffith/Narrandera route. The second 340A followed a month later.

The two 340Bs arrived in October 1990, and they entered service on the routes between Sydney and Dubbo, Griffith, Narrandera, Broken Hill, Orange and Albury, using Sydney as the base. Hazelton now serves 37 destinations with its fleet of 13 Navajos, one Bandeirante, one Beech 1900, two SD-360s and two Saab 340Bs (the 340As have been returned).

During the last four years, Hazelton has seen a spectacular growth in passenger boardings. In the year ending June 1988 it carried 63,401; the following year 105,106. Then it jumped to 172,350, and in the year ending June 1991 Hazelton Airlines expects to carry about 210,000 passengers. During the same period the number of destinations has increased from 20 to 35 and staff from 74 to 201.

Saab 340 Fleet

VH-OLG	019	Apr.90/Apr.91	Leased from PLM
VH-OLH	069	May 90/Oct.90	Leased from LAPA
VH-OLM	205	Oct.90/	(340B) 'New Horizons'
VH-OLN	207	Oct.90/	(340B)

Hazelton's first 340B overflying Sydney harbour *(Saab)*

JAPAN AIR SYSTEM (JN)   Japan

Japan Air System (JAS) is today the third largest Japanese airline. It was formerly known as Toa Domestic but changed its name in 1988 when it launched its first international route. Toa Domestic was formed in 1971 through the merger of Japan Domestic Airlines and Toa Airways. Based in Tokyo, it today operates a large fleet of aircraft consisting of A300s, DC-10s, MD-80s and DC-9-40s, as well as nearly 30 YS-11s. They mostly fly domestic routes but since 1988 also operate a few international services. Eight 747-400s and ten MD-90s are on order. Today it serves 38 cities in Japan, carrying a million passengers per month as well as to Seoul and Singapore from Tokyo.

In 1983 JAS formed together with the local government, a subsidiary called Japan Air Commuter, now based in Kagoshima (until 1988 it was based in Amami Oshima). JAS has 60 per cent of the shares and the local government the remaining 40 per cent. The intention was to provide a scheduled air-service in the Amami Islands. Its first aircraft were two new Dornier 228s, later a third was added. During 1988, Japan Air System started transferring some YS-11s to its subsidiary along with loss making routes. By 1991 this fleet had grown to six aircraft. With the average age of these aircraft approaching 20 years, a replacement aircraft was needed. Consequently, an order was concluded with Saab for eight 340Bs, plus four options, in March 1990. Configured with 36 seats, these aircraft

are scheduled for delivery from the first quarter of 1992. JAS has become the third 340 customer (after Crossair and AMR) to order its own Saab 340, simulator for delivery in 1993.

When the 340s arrive, they will replace the YS-11s on the routes from Kagoshima to Tanega–Shima, Yaku–Jima, Okinoerabu-Shima and Yoron–Jima. They are also expected to open up new routes. The Do.228s will continue to provide services between the Amami Islands. The 340Bs will be based in Kagoshima.

Founding President of Japan Air Commuter was Hiroshi Hamada, and in 1989 it had 135 employees. Passenger boardings for 1989 were 244,000, a 83.5 per cent increase from the previous year. New President (since June 1991) is Yoshitomi Ono.

Saab 340B Fleet

JA	-92
JA	-92
JA	-93
JA	-93
JA	-93
JA	-94
JA	-94
JA	-94

An artist impression of the JAS 340B *(Saab/A. Sturgess)*

KELLY SPRINGFIELD

USA

Kelly Springfield is a large American tyre company, a subsidiary of Goodyear, and based in Cumberland, Maryland. In April 1985 it signed an order for one corporate Saab 340 to replace its Beech King Air 200. It needed a larger aircraft than the King Air but wanted to keep operating costs down, hence a large turboprop aircraft like the 340. It also operates a Lear Jet 55 for longer distance requirements.

The aircraft was outfitted with an executive interior for 19 passengers by Fairchild in San Antonio, and delivered to Kelly Springfield in October 1986. It is actually owned by the Maryland Department of Transport, but leased to Kelly Springfield.

Kelly Springfield does all maintenance of the aircraft itself at its operating base in Cumberland, where the Lear Jet is also based.

The 340 mainly flies from Cumberland to Pittsburgh, for the passengers to connect with scheduled airlines, and then it usually flies on to Akron, Ohio, where Kelly Springfield has another plant. This trajectory is flown up to four times per day. It also regularly flies to Freeport, Illinois; Fayetteville, North Carolina and occasionally to Tyler, Texas; all these places also have Kelly Springfield plants. Other regular destinations are Miami and Phoenix.

Average loads are eight passengers, and the yearly utilization is around 1,000 hours which is high for an executive aircraft.

Although Kelly Springfield does not have any current plans to buy any more executive Saabs, it plans to use their current aircraft for many years to come.

Saab 340A Fleet

N44KS	050	Oct.86/

Kelly Springfield's single 340A *(E. Gual/Aviation Photography of Miami)*

KENDELL AIRLINES (KD)   Australia

Kendell Airlines was set up in 1966, then known as PremiAir, by Donald Kendell, who remains Managing Director of the airline. Don Kendell has a background as a pilot with BEA flying DC-3s and Viscounts. His first aircraft was a Piper Apache which he used for air-taxi work. It was later joined by a Cherokee Six. In 1971 he began scheduled services, now under the name Kendell Airlines, from Wagga Wagga to Melbourne with a Piper Navajo. This route had been dropped by Ansett, and Kendell now saw an opportunity to exploit. More routes were soon added. The Navajos were replaced by DH.114 Herons in 1975 which remained until 1981 when the Metros took over. The first had arrived two year's earlier. Kendell worked closely with **Ansett** from the beginning, and as such has benefitted greatly from Ansett's decision to cut back on regional routes. TNT/News Corp, the owner of Ansett, had a minority shareholding in the airline but this was later increased to 70 per cent. As Ansett dropped routes, Kendell picked them up and gradually expanded. The biggest transfer was in 1986 when Ansett closed down the Airlines of South Australia operation. Kendell took over the routes from Adelaide to Mount Gambier, Streaky Bay, Ceduna, Port Lincoln, Whyalla and Broken Hill. In one jump, Kendell doubled its number of passengers. Ansett had been using Fokker F27s which were too large for the available traffic. Today the airline caters mainly for business people, and is known as the 'Country Connection'. Wagga Wagga continues to be the main base, but Kendell has also set up bases at Melbourne and Adelaide. Ansett continues to provide all handling and bookings.

Kendell was an early Saab 340 customer. The first aircraft was ordered in July 1984 and delivered in February the following year. The second was bought in 1985, followed by a third and a fourth aircraft in 1987 and 1988. All these were delivered new from the factory; a fifth 340 was purchased from the bankrupt Air Limousin in 1990.

During 1989–1990, Kendell added three destinations. It took over the Adelaide–Kingscote route from Lloyd Aviation on October 1 1990, and after Ansett withdrew their Fokker F-50s, Kendell took over the Melbourne–Burnie/Wynyard route in October 1989. Finally it took over the Melbourne–Devonport service one month later.

Kendell today serves over 20 destinations with its fleet of eight Metros and five Saab 340s. It has 178 employees and carried 262,000 passengers in 1989. For the financial year ending June 1990, it carried over 300,000 passengers. Its top route is Adelaide–Port Lincoln where 74,734 passengers were carried in 1990. TNT/News Corp now owns 100 per cent of Kendell, after they purchased the remaining 30 per cent from Don Kendell in October 1990.

Saab 340A Fleet

VH-EKD	155	Aug.89/	'City of Wagga Wagga'
VH-EKT	085	Mar.90/	Ex ALTA, 'City of Burnie'
VH-KDI	131	Nov.88/	'City of Whyalla'
VH-KDK	016	Mar.85/	'City of Mt. Gambier'
VH-KDP	052	May 86/	'City of Broken Hill'

A Kendell 340A overflying Australian bushland (*Saab*)

KLM CITYHOPPER (WU/HN)   Holland

The origins of KLM Cityhopper is NetherLines which was founded by Leen Jansson, a Dutch architect, in 1984. Initially this airline was known simply as CASH (Commuter Air Services Holland) but was renamed **NetherLines** before it started operations. On January 8 1985, it began operations with two BAe Jetstream 31s. By Mid-1985 this fleet had grown to four, of which three flew the scheduled routes from Amsterdam to Groningen, Enschede, Osnabrück, Luxembourg and Strasbourg. The fourth was dedicated to charter. The start of the airline was the culmination of two years preparations and fund raisings.

The Jetstream fleet grew to six aircraft during spring-1986. NetherLines was then serving ten points in Holland and abroad. These were Birmingham and Luton in England, Groningen, Enschede and Eindhoven in Holland, Cologne in Germany, Vienna in Austria, Luxembourg, and Strasbourg in France. Staff had grown to 100.

Initial headquarters were in Rotterdam, but this later moved to Eindhoven and NetherLines worked closely with KLM from the beginning. Its schedule was linked into KLM's reservation system. At this time it started evaluating 30-seat aircraft. At a board-meeting in April 1987 it decided to lease a Saab 340A from Norway. It was delivered in June 1987 and entered service on the Amsterdam–Luxembourg–Strasbourg–Amsterdam and Amsterdam–Bristol–Cardiff–Amsterdam routes.

By this time, the airline had been sold to the Nedlloyd group, who also owned Transavia. However this ownership was shortlived. On March 25 1988, KLM announced that they intended to buy NetherLines from Nedlloyd. The intention was to merge NetherLines with KLM's own regional airline, NLM, which operated F-27s and F-28s.

KLM reaffirmed the NetherLine choice of the Saab 340, by signing a firm order for six Saab 340Bs on October 10 1988. At the same time KLM ordered seven Fokker 50s to replace the F-27s. Meanwhile NetherLines would lease another two 340As as interim aircraft. These aircraft would also sport the NetherLines livery. They were delivered during spring 1989.

During 1989 KLM restructured the NLM and NetherLines organisations. They soon decided to expand the original network of 25 destinations to 40. As a consequence of this they placed follow-on orders with both Fokker and Saab, ordering four more 340Bs. Before the year was finished another two 340s had been ordered, making 12 in total.

The merger of NLM and NetherLines into a new regional airline with a new corporate identity took longer than originally envisaged. Consequently when KLM took delivery of its first 340B in January 1990, it was unable to present its new corporate identity. Hence the first aircraft were delivered all white! During the spring of 1990 the new joint NLM/NetherLines was renamed 'KLM Cityhopper' and a new paint scheme was unveiled. However the airline did not officially become KLM Cityhopper until April 1991.

The 340Bs arrived at a quick pace; by June 1990 eight were in service and new destinations were added. The 340As were returned and the last two Jetstreams were handed back to BAe in April 1990. The first F-50 arrived during August.

In May 1990 KLM launched a new service from Amsterdam to Malmö.

In the winter timetable 1990–91 KLM Cityhopper flew the 340s to the following destinations from Amsterdam: Malmö, Hanover, Stuttgart, Luxembourg, Strasbourg, London (Luton), Birmingham, Nuremberg, Cardiff, Bristol, Basle/Mulhouse and Southampton. November saw the launch of a new service to Dresden. The 340s are also employed on domestic routes to Rotterdam, Eindhoven and Maastricht, and from these on to Paris and Hamburg. Maintenance is carried out by KLM Helicopters.

The managing director of KLM Cityhopper is Anton Leyer, and in the fiscal year of 1990 NLM carried 700,000 passengers and NetherLines 100,000.

Saab 340A Fleet

PH-KJH	055	Jun.87/May 90	Leased from Salenia
PH-KJK	008	Feb.89/Sep.91	Leased from Saab
PH-KJL	037	Mar.89/Apr.90	Leased from Salenia

Saab 340B Fleet

PH-KSA	175	Jan.90/
PH-KSB	178	Feb.90/
PH-KSC	179	Mar.90/
PH-KSD	183	May 90/
PH-KSE	186	Apr.90/
PH-KSF	188	Apr.90/
PH-KSG	189	May 90/
PH-KSH	195	Jun.90/
PH-KSI	217	Nov.90/
PH-KSK	226	Feb.91/
PH-KSL	270	Nov.91/
PH-KSM		92

The three 340As were painted in the NetherLines livery, as shown on the previous page PH-KJH photographed at Luxembourg Airport *(Author)*

All 340Bs carry the new KLM Cityhopper livery as below *(S.A.P.)*

LAER (?)
Argentina

LAER, or 'Lineas Aereas Entre Rios' as its full name reads, is based in Parana, province of Entre Rios in north eastern Argentina. LAER is owned by the provincial government.

It was originally set up in the late 1960s to operate scheduled regional air services using some of the government owned aircraft such as Cessna 337s. It was at this time known as 'LAPER', Lineas Aereas Provinciales de Entre Rios. By early 1970s, two Cessna 402s had joined the fleet.

In 1973 two locally manufactured IA-50 Guaranis were purchased from the Air Force-owned aircraft factory in Cordoba. These unpressurised aircraft could carry 15 passengers. However, in 1979 the company was disbanded.

In 1986 it was relaunched as LAER with the IA-50 aircraft plus a couple of Cessna 402s. The routes flown were Parana–Buenos Aires and Concordia–Gualeguaychu–Buenos Aires. The following year a Saab 340A was ordered, and delivered in November. However, local authorisations held up the entry into service of the aircraft, and

it was thus wet-leased to ALFA for two months from February 1988. It was also used as a VIP aircraft by the provincial government. ALFA's economic problems prevented it from extending the lease. By now LAER had received necessary permits and the aircraft entered service on the daily Parana–Buenos Aires route on April 4 1988.

Mounting economic problems for the Entre Rios province prevented it from continuing to subsidise the LAER operation which due to low fares continued to loose money. Consequently, LAER was forced to return their flag-ship to Saab in September 1989. LAER reverted to their old IA-50 aircraft to continue their operations at a much reduced scale.

Saab 340A Fleet

LV-AXW	106	Nov.87/Sep.89	Returned to Saab

LAER's single 340A overflying Parana *(Author)*

LAPA (MJ)   Argentina

LAPA, or Lineas Aereas Privadas Argentinas SA as its full name reads, was founded in December 1977 by Count Claudio von Thyssen. The intention was to fly regional routes from Buenos Aires, and for this purpose three Metro IIs were purchased. Its first scheduled service was flown on January 22 1978, on the La Plata–Pehuajo route. Meanwhile LAPA tried to obtain traffic rights from Buenos Aires, and these were finally given in March 1979. The Metros were then sold and three secondhand YS-11s purchased instead. These aircraft mainly flew regional routes within the Buenos Aires province.

LAPA made the headlines in June 1980 when they announced an order for three BAe.146s for delivery in 1982, and the intention to lease BAC-111s until the BAe.146 arrived. At the same time they applied for trunk routes within Argentina. However, they soon ran into difficulties, and the order was converted into options by early 1981 and soon after cancelled altogether.

Instead, LAPA bought two new SD-330s from Shorts in 1980 which were delivered the same year. With the fuel crisis of the early 1980s, the YS-11s became unprofitable on LAPA routes and were sold in 1982. Before departing they inaugurated LAPA's first international route, from Buenos Aires to Colonia in Uruguay.

In September 1984, Count von Thyssen sold the airline to the current owner, Andrew Deutsch, a prominent Argentine/American businessman whose main business is a large supermarket chain.

Deutsch reorganized the airline and decided to concentrate on regional routes. A third 330 was acquired in January 1985. In December the same year it leased a Bandeirante for some of the smaller routes, but the venture was not profitable, and the aircraft was soon returned and the routes dropped.

Instead it started evaluating a replacement for the 330s and soon picked the 340. An order for two Saab 340s was signed on November 18 1986. Both aircraft were delivered during spring 1987 and the first 340 entered service on April 21, on the Buenos Aires–General Pico route. Other destinations were Tandil, Necochea as well as Colonia. During the summer season it also flew to Villa Gessell and Santa Teressita on the Atlantic coast. During 1987 LAPA carried 53,765 passengers.

In 1988 LAPA signed an agreement with **Aerolineas Argentinas** to fly a number of routes in co-operation with the Argentine flag carrier. These were from Cordoba to Catamarca, La Rioja, Rio Cuarto, and flying from Buenos Aires via Rosario to Cordoba. LAPA also inaugurated a second international route from Rosario to Montevideo, the capital of Uruguay. Traffic increased in 1988 to 68,924 passengers.

Late 1989 saw the economic climate of Argentina yet again taking a nose-dive, LAPA cut back its network and concentrated on Colonia, Gral Pico and Cordoba. Consequently, one 340 became surplus and was temporarily leased, via Saab, to Hazelton and later Air Nelson.

Saab 340A Fleet

N69LP	069	Apr.87/Mar.90	Leased out, ret. Jul.91
N72LP	072	Apr.87/	

LAPA's 340 overflying the down-town airport of Buenos Aires, its home-base (Saab/N. Pealing)

MANX AIRLINES (JE)   United Kingdom

Manx was formed in 1982. Originally BMA and Air UK owned 75 per cent and 25 per cent respectively and intention was to develop a scheduled air service from the Isle of Man. (BMA assumed full control in 1988). Manx operates as an independent airline within the Airlines of Britain Group together with Loganair. Operations began on November 1. Initial routes were from the Isle of Man to Belfast, Blackpool, Dublin, Edinburgh, Glasgow, Liverpool, London (Heathrow) and Manchester.

Aircraft equipment has varied during Manx's history. Initially it used a single Twin Otter, two Fokker F-27s and a Shorts 330. Soon a Viscount 800 joined the fleet as well as SD-360s. These aircraft became the mainstay of the fleet.

In 1986 Manx decided to replace the SD-360 with a Saab 340 on the Liverpool–London (Heathrow) route. One 340 was leased from Saab in November, and entered service on December 3. It flew the Heathrow service five times a day during the week, and on weekends to the Isle of Man. Both routes were from Liverpool where the aircraft was based. Maintenance was done by McAlpine at Luton Airport who had been designated a 340 service centre for the UK by Saab. However traffic grew rapidly on these two routes, and consequently Manx decided to acquire a larger aircraft. The 340 was returned to Saab in October 1988 and replaced by a BAe.146-100. The Viscount 800 was replaced by BAe.ATP in 1989.

Number of employees is about 300, and the Managing Director is Terry Liddiard. Manx carried 506,000 passengers in 1989. The present fleet is one BAe.146-100, three BAe.ATPs (one leased to British Airways) and three SD-360s.

During spring 1991, Manx set up a new hub in Cardiff with two second-hand Jetstream 31s.

Saab 340A Fleet

G-HOPP   008   Nov.86/Oct.88

Manx single 340A overflying Liverpool *(Saab/N. Pealing)*

MELLON BANK
USA

Mellon is a large American bank with over 18,000 employees at 652 domestic locations, mainly in north eastern, mid-Atlantic and upper midwestern states.

In 1983 it ordered one executive Saab 340 to replace a Sabreliner 60. This 340 was fitted out for 16 passengers by Fairchild in San Antonio, and handed over to Mellon on November 22 1985. Mellon thus became the first operator of an executive 340. Prior to this it had briefly used Fairchild's 340 demonstrator. It was later equipped with an APU by Duncan Aviation in Lincoln, Nebraska. Its base was Allegheny County Airport in Pittsburgh, Pennsylvania. Along with the 340, Mellon also operated a six-passenger Sabreliner 65. The 340 was used for the shorter sectors, up to 2.5 hours flying time. About 85 per cent of the trips were to Philadelphia, Washington DC, Harrisburg, New York (Newark) and Cleveland.

Average passenger loads were about 4.5.

During 1987, Mellon Bank, like many US financial institutions suffered a downturn in business. Consequently the Sabreliner 65 was sold and the 340 kept. However the management re-evaluated their corporate aircraft requirements and after having sold the Sabreliner, they later decided to sell the 340 as well. It was offered for sale during the summer of 1988 and was sold to **Great American Insurance**.

Saab 340A Fleet
N19M   022   Nov.85/Aug.88
Reregistered N53LB with Gr. Am. Insurance Oct.88

Mellon's single 340A featured a discreet livery *(J. Wegg)*

METRO AIRLINES (AA)

USA

The original Metro Airlines was founded in 1967 as 'Houston Metro' operating as a Continental Airline's commuter. Initial fleet consisted of three DHC-6 Twin Otters, with a fourth added in 1969. The route was a 15 minute flight from a stolport near NASA Space Center to Houston International Airport. The stolport was closed in 1974, but Metro relocated to Dallas (Fort Worth). In the same year Edward Henderson purchased Metro for $3 million.

Later when Continental entered some financial difficulties, Metro switched to Eastern. However this partnership did not last for long. Despite the changes the Twin Otter fleet continued to grow during the 1970s, by 1977 12 were in service operating both from Houston as Metro Airlines (HY) and from Dallas as Metroflight Airlines (FY). In 1979 another two Twin Otters were added, but they were soon too small. Consequently Metro ordered five new SD-330s late 1978.

These entered service late 1979 and early 1980. The following year another four Twin Otters, two SD-330s and the first four CV-580s joined Metro. In October 1981 the company went public. Traffic increased steadily and in 1982 Metro carried 697,563 passengers.

The close relationship with Eastern led them to ask Metro to set up a feeder in Atlanta. Metro did so in 1984 by creating a new separate organisation called 'Eastern Metro Express' and ordered new Jetstream 31s from BAe.

Meanwhile **American Airlines** was building up a hub at Dallas (Fort Worth) Airport and needed a feeder airline. When American set up its American Eagle organisation in 1984 it asked Metro to set up a feeder in Dallas. For this purpose, Metro created a new airline called 'Metro Express II'. With two out of ten Jetstream 31s ordered, Metro Express II began operations on March 15 1985 to Wichita Fall.

Finally in 1985 Eastern asked Metro to set up a feeder in San Juan, which it did (for futher information see Aviation Associates).

All these regionals are controlled by a holding company 'Metro Airlines Inc', whose President and CEO is Jay Seaborn. Chairman is Edward Henderson. Each airline is run as a separate profit centre.

Meanwhile the main fleet continued to grow. By 1984 15 Twin Otters, seven SD-330s and five CV-580s were in Texas while another Twin Otter was in San Juan. The Atlanta operation was gearing up for its first 12 Jetstream 31s. Including the Eastern Metro Express, Metro carried 844,839 passengers ranking Metro as number six of the top 50 regional airlines in USA.

Delta's feeder in Dallas was Rio Airways but after they filed for Chapter 11, Rio was replaced by ASA which began operations in Dallas in December 1986. Meanwhile Metro Express II started flying most of the old Rio routes for American. Traffic gains took a big jump, in 1986 Metro carried 1,493,981, making it the largest US regional airline after Air Wisconsin.

In Dallas Metro expanded rapidly as American built up its hub. By 1987 Metroflight had a fleet of 16 CV-580s while Metro Express II had a fleet of ten Jetstream 31s and four SD-330s. All Twin Otters had been sold or transferred to San Juan.

To replace the CV-580s, Metro placed an order for 16 Saab 340As with the option on another ten in April 1987. At that time, it was the largest single order ever received by Saab. The 340s started arriving in August, and all 16 were delivered by July 1988 enabling all CV-580s to be withdrawn from service. Metroflight was then serving eight cities from Dallas. At the same time Metro Express II served five cities with ten Jetstream 31s and four SD-330s.

In August 1987, Metro purchased Abilene, Tex. based Chaparral Airlines for $5.7 million. Chaparral served Alexandria and Shreveport from Dallas, and Austin, San Antonio and Laredo from Abilene. The fleet consisted of four CASA 212 and three Gulfstream G-1C. At this time the three Dallas based operations carried 100,000 passengers per month. Chaparral was later merged with Metro Express II under the Chaparral name. At the same time a new airline was set up in 1988, called 'Starlight Express'. With SD-330s it started flying cargo only.

By late 1988 the 16 Saab 340A's were serving nine cities out of Dallas (Fort Worth). These were, from the north down, Springfield, Fayetteville, Fort Smith, Lawton (also the maintenance base for all 340s), Longview, Tyler, Beaumont, Lake Charle and Lafayette.

Traffic continued to increase, so Metro converted its ten options into a firm order for ten Saab 340Bs in January 1989. These were delivered between November 1989 and December 1990. During 1989 Metro purchased Brockway in New England, and renamed it Metro Northeast (see Brockway).

In 1989 Metroflight carried 825,000 passengers while Chaparral carried 580,000 and Eastern Metro 403,000. The following year Chaparral was merged with Metroflight creating a single operation in Dallas. Total boardings for the combined operation were 1,234,185 in 1990.

However, during 1990 Metro began to feel the effects of Eastern's problems. This in combination with the oil price increases and other effects of the Gulf crisis, caused a $15.55 million loss for the third quarter ending January 31 1991. When Eastern ceased operations on January 18 1991, Metro was forced to shut down its operation at Atlanta. But the financial problems persisted, and on February 7, Metro closed Metro Northeast, and in the same month sold Aviation Associates in Puerto Rico.

Metro continued its remaining operation in Texas, but was forced to declare Chapter 11 on April 2 1991. The company is currently being reorganized but the operations continue with traffic continuing to grow in the Dallas hub area. Metro is today the only independent American Eagle carrier left.

Saab 340A Fleet

N360MA	089	Aug.87/	Leased M. Northeast Jan.90/Nov.90
N361MA	091	Aug.87/	Leased M. Northeast Jan.90/Nov.90
N362MA	095	Sep.87/	
N363MA	098	Sep.87/	
N364MA	099	Sep.87/	
N365MA	102	Oct.87/	
N366MA	103	Oct.87/	
N367MA	107	Nov.87/	
N368MA	109	Dec.87/	
N369MA	110	Dec.87/	
N370MA	112	Feb.88/	
N371MA	114	Feb.88/	
N372MA	115	Mar.88/	
N373MA	118	May 88/	
N374MA	119	May 88/	
N375MA	123	Jun.88/	

Saab 340B Fleet

N586MA	165	Nov.89/
N587MA	166	Dec.89/
N588MA	169	Dec.89/
N589MA	172	Dec.89/
N590MA	181	Apr.90/
N591MA	192	Jun.90/
N592MA	199	Jul.90/
N593MA	206	Oct.90/
N594MA	212	Nov.90/
N595MA	216	Dec.90/

Opposite, a Metro 340 taxying at its Dallas (Forth Worth) base *(Author)*

NORVING (RT)   Norway

Norving can trace its history back to 1959. On July 24 of that year, A/s Varangfly was founded. It started scheduled operations the following year from Kirkenes to Bardufoss and Ivalo. In April 1971 the company changed name to A/s Varangfly-Norwings after merging with Norwings A/s in Tromsö. A second name change to simply Norving took place the subsequent year after Nordlandsfly in Bodö was absorbed.

Norving has, over the years, operated many different types of aircraft, including Cessna 206s, DHC Beavers, BN2A Islanders, Piper Navajos and Cessna 404s. It was an early customer for Dornier 228s, the first three arrived in 1983, and four more followed at yearly intervals. Two Metro III and two Beech 99 also saw service with the airline.

Norving was a private company owned by banks, industrialists, insurance companies and around 2,600 private investors. The corporate headquarter is in Kirkenes.

On September 26 1983, Norving signed an order for three Saab 340As with deliveries starting in 1985. The first 340 entered service in February 1986 on the Skien–Stavanger route. In the first year of 340 operations, Norving flew 150,000 scheduled passengers. Operations were from two main bases, Skien and Trondheim with 340s based at both. Main 340 routes were from Skien to Stavanger, Bergen, Oslo and Trondheim.

During 1987 Norving encountered serious financial problems and was forced to cut back its operations. Another Norwegian regional airline, Norsk Air, took over many routes. One of the 340s was leased from JB Aviation and this aircraft was returned in early 1988. During the same time Norving gave up all routes in southern Norway and disposed of most of its fleet. The last 340 service was flown on February 29 1988, after which the aircraft was leased out and eventually sold. Norving maintains a small operation in northern Norway.

Saab 340A Fleet

LN-NVD	037	Dec.85/Oct.88	Sold JB, Salenia
LN-NVE	055	Jun.86/Oct.88	Sold JB, Salenia
LN-NVF	087	Jun.87/Feb.88	Leased from JB Aviation

Norving's livery was a copy of the Swedair colours enabling the two carriers to interchange aircraft (Saab)

PHILIP MORRIS

USA

This major American consumer goods company (Miller Brewing, 7-up, Gillette, tobacco and food products) operates a large fleet of corporate aircraft. It ordered three Saab 340s in executive configuration plus one option in March 1983. The purchase was completed through the local distributor Teterboro Aircraft who had ordered six corporate 340s for resale in the eastern region of USA. The third 340 and the option were sold back to FAC in November 1985. The other two were delivered to Philip Morris during spring 1986 after having been fitted out with a 14 seat executive interior by Fairchild in San Antonio, Texas. They were also unique in being fitted with an APU in the rear fuselage. At Philip Morris they replaced the Gulfstream G-1s. Both were based in Richmond, Virginia, where all maintenance was carried out.

While in service with Philip Morris the 340s mainly flew the daily shuttle service from Richmond to Louisville, Kentucky and Charlotte, South Carolina. Other regular destinations were Teterboro outside New York, Houston and Chicago. Occasional visits were made to Miami and Toronto, Canada.

In February 1991 the 340s were withdrawn from service, and replaced by the BAe.125-800. One 340 has been sold while the other is currently for sale.

Saab 340A Fleet

N100PM	029	Mar.86/Feb.91	For Sale
N200PM	036	Apr.86/Feb.91	Sold AMP Apr.91 as N77M

As the other corporate 340's, the Philip Morris aircraft featured a discreet livery (E.Chernoff)

SAAB SCANIA   Sweden

Saab utilized the first four 340 for the flight test programme which lead to the type certificate in May 1984. The prototype was subsequently mounted on a pole outside Linköping when the city celebrated its 700 anniversary.

The second prototype has been retained for the subsequent flight-testing including the 340B certification. It is currently being used in preparation for the Saab 2000 flight test programme.

The third 340, was a pre-production aircraft. It was subsequently modified by Fairchild to incorporate an APU. It was later cut up, and various pieces used for the Saab 2000 programme. The last aircraft was the first production standard, and was later delivered to Comair.

Saab attempted to sell the 340 as a corporate aircraft, but only sold four 340As. For this marketing campaign the Saab office in USA actually operated a corporate demonstrator during 1985 and 1986. As the sales-result could not warrant an exclusive demonstrator, it was sold and later converted to airliner standard for Comair.

Saab 340A Fleet

SE-ISF	001	Jan.83/May 85	Preserved
SE-ISA	002	May 83/	Current
SE-ISB	003	Aug.83/Sep.86	Withdrawn
SE-E04	004	Mar.84/Oct.84	To Comair
N340SF	014	Nov.84/Nov.87	To Comair

Below, second prototype SE-ISA photographed while flying in Spain *(Saab)*

Previous page, N340SF was the corporate demonstrator used on the American market *(Saab/N. Pealing)*

SALAIR (YD)   Sweden

The forerunner of Salair is AMA Air Express which was founded in Gothenburg in 1976. Its first aircraft was a Cessna 402 and its first route was Gothenburg–Linköping which was started in January 1979. In 1980 it added Ronneby and Kalmar while two more Cessna 402s arrived. Växsjö became a new destination in 1981, and the following year the Linköping route was extended to Stockholm (Bromma). At the same time it introduced Metro IIs. Also briefly served was Alborg in Denmark. In 1982 20,000 passengers were carried, and in the following year 30,000.

In October 1985 **Norving** in Norway acquired 75 per cent of the company, but the general manager Ola Falnäs stayed on. Plans were drawn up to build a new hangar in Gothenburg and open up new routes to Skien in Norway and Copenhagen via Halmstad. However Norving's financial problems soon forced its Swedish subsidiary into bankruptcy on October 15. Salenia, the Swedish shipping company then became involved. Late 1986 it took over AMA Air Express, and as of January 26 1987, it became known as Salair. Its new general manager was Urmas Kruusval.

In order to start replacing the Metros, Salair ordered two Saab 340As in March 1987, with an option on a third. The first 340 was delivered in September the same year. It entered service on the Linköping–Stockholm route on September 17.

The other forerunner to today's Salair is **Skyways**. It had been operating scheduled services since 1979 with Skyvans and later Metros. Its main route was Stockholm–Gävle–Mora, and later Gothenburg–Malmö. On October 22 1987, it ordered one Saab 340A for their Mora route. However, the airline was purchased by Salenia in March 1988 before the aircraft was delivered.

A new hangar and head office was inaugurated at Gothenburg (Landvetter) Airport in September 1988. At the same time Salair announced an order for another two 340s, adding to the three it already purchased, (one of these was later cancelled). during the same year, Salenia purchased 25 per cent of the new airline, **Air Bremen**, and the fourth 340A was leased directly to this airline. When the second 340 was delivered in October it was put into service on the Stockholm-Gävle–Mora route. The third 340 soon followed and was put into service on the Linköping–Gothenburg as well as Stockholm route. Passenger boardings during 1988 were 165,000.

However Salair continued to lose money. Consequently the less successful routes from Gothenburg to Kalmar, Ronneby, Linköping and Malmö were quietly dropped. Instead Salair decided to move its headquarters to Linköping and concentrate on the routes out of Linköping. A new hangar and head-office was inaugurated in June 1989 at the 'Saab' airfield in Linköping. In October Per Töörn was appointed as new general manager. At this time Salair had 80 employees and it carried 128,624 passengers during 1989. The last Metros were also phased out.

After a long battle, Salair got the approval to start flying from Linköping to Copenhagen, the first flight taking place on April 3 1989.

In the same year Salenia purchased Malmö Aviation with its fleet of BAe.146s and FH-227/F-27s. This company flies mostly cargo and charter. However in October 1990 Malmö Aviation began a new service from Malmö to Hamburg, its first scheduled route.

Late in 1990 Salenia negotiated with ABA to merge Salair with Swedair. However, after several months of negotiations, the talks were discontinued in February 1991 and instead Salenia began negotiations to merge Salair with Avia in Norrköping. This time the negotiations were successful, and the two companies merged under the 'Avia' name in July 1991. Avia's Shorts aircraft will be replaced with Saab 340s.

Meanwhile, Salair is consolidating its present network. Having added a fourth 340 it now flies to Mora six times per weekday, seven times per weekday to Stockholm and four times per weekday to Copenhagen. The Hamburg route is flown twice daily.

Salair's Saab 340A Fleet

SE-ISK	100	Sep.87/	'Blåklinten'
LN-SAA	130	Oct.88/	'Ängsklockan'
SE-ISM	133	Nov.88/	'Kaprifolen'
SE-KRN	159	No.90/	Ex Air Bremen

Salenia owned 340s

SE-KPD	037	Nov.88/	Leased KLM, Express A/L
SE-KPE	055	Nov.88/	Leased KLM, Express A/L
SE-KSI	223	Jan.91/	Leased Express A/L
SE-KSK	229	Feb.91/	

Salair introduced a highly visible livery with the arrival of the 340s (Saab)

SÜDAVIA (FV)
Germany

Südavia was set up in Munich during 1984, initially operating a single Beech King Air. This was quickly followed by another King Air and a leased Dornier 228. As traffic grew, a need for a 19 seater soon became apparent and Südavia chose the Beech 1900, becoming one of the first operators of this type in Europe. The B-1900 soon settled in on its routes from Munich to Saarbrucken, Strasbourg, Pisa and Verona.

The B-1900 fleet grew to three aircraft and as traffic continued to grow, Südavia began evaluating 30-seat aircraft. As a consequence of DLT becoming a shareholder, Südavia leased two Brasilias. When DLT decided to phase out the Brasilia from its fleet and lease the aircraft to Midway, Südavia began evaluating the Saab 340. During 1989 it carried 38,000 passengers.

In December 1989, **Alphalines** (see separate entry) became a new shareholder, acquiring 44 per cent of the company, and plans were made to introduce up to four 340s. Hans Schneider, the original founder, kept 51 per cent. He reappointed Rolf Kasebier as general manager. Applications were made for new routes to Paris from Saarbrucken and from Munich to Dresden.

The first 340 entered service in February 1990 on the routes from Munich to Saarbrucken and Geneva. The second 340 was never delivered since by that time Alphalines had become alarmed at the financial position of Südavia. The remaining two B-1900s flew the remaining routes from Saarbrucken to Hamburg and Dusseldorf.

However, financial problems mounted, and on March 31 1990, Südavia suspended operations. In the following two months, various unsuccessful attempts were made to find fresh capital, but on May 23, Südavia was finally closed down. The B-1900 were returned to the Beech distributor in Augsburg (owned by Mr Schneider) and the 340 joined its sister at Air Exel in Belgium.

Saab 340B Fleet

HB-AHZ	163	Feb.90/Mar.90
HB-AHY	171	Never entered service

Südavia never had time to repaint the 340s, hence the Air Exel livery *(A. Härry)*

SWEDAIR (JG)

Sweden

Swedair was founded on October 5 1935, as 'Svensk Flygtjänst AB' by Tor Eliasson, then only 21 years old. First aircraft was an Avro Avian imported from England. Initial operations were mostly flight-school activities but also ad-hoc charter, and air photography. During the war, target towing started, an activity that was to grow and continue for many years to come. More aircraft were added, amongst these Bücker Jungmann, DH60 Moth, and Junkers W33 equipment.

During the 1950s, the target towing expanded and 19 Fairey Firefly's were purchased from England plus 17 Saab B-17s from the Swedish Air Force. Later on, Douglas Skyraiders and Gloster Meteors were used. A separate base for this was set up in Vidsel in northern Sweden in 1957.

In 1952-53 a new maintenance base was formed in Malmö for contract maintenance.

Another activity was representing foreign manufacturers. Early agencies were for Bücker in Germany, Scottish Aviation, Cessna (all types), Lockheed (Hercules), Beagle and many equipment manufacturers.

Svensk Flygtjänst also tried their hands on charter flights. In 1958 it purchased two Beech 18s and two Lockheed Lodestars. About this time it started using the name 'Swedair' for such flights. Plans for incorporating large aircraft such as Douglas DC-6Bs were not fulfilled. The Lodestar was also used for calibration of navigational aides on behalf of the Swedish aviation authorities. Later on, a Douglas DC-3 was employed for this task.

Scheduled air service came late in the history of Swedair. On December 20 1974, Svensk Flygtjänst merged with state owned Crownair (founded 1968) and the new company became known as 'Swedair AB'. Ownership was split 50 per cent between the Ministry of Defense, and 25 per cent each to ABA (Swedish holding company for SAS) and Linjeflyg. Crownair was at this time operating three Twin Otters on behalf of Linjeflyg and this fleet quickly grew to eight aircraft. In February 1983 Swedair purchased Aerocenter, a small Swedish charter airline with two Fairchild F-27s. Three more F-27s were acquired and put on SAS and **Linjeflyg** services.

During 1980 Swedair started evaluating a replacement aircraft for the Twin Otters. The DHC-8, E-120 and Saab 340 were considered, and the latter aircraft chosen. A preliminary agreement for seven 340s was signed in the autumn of 1980. The final contract, which had by now grown to ten aircraft, was signed on February 26 1981, by Karl-Erik Strand, who had just been appointed as the new general manager of Swedair. The intention was that seven of these aircraft would be used on Linjeflyg routes.

The first 340 was accepted in December 1984, and placed into service on January 6 on the Stockholm-Borlänge route. When the second aircraft arrived, it was placed into service on January 21 on the Kramfors route. The third opened up the Trollhättan route on February 4.

After this followed a gap until the next batch of 340s arrived late 1985 and early 1986. These were all placed into service in the northern part of Sweden. The fourth 340 began the Luleå–Gällivare route in October and the fifth began the Gällivare–Luleå–Umeå–Sundsvall service on December 1st.

The sixth went to the Borlänge service and the seventh to the network in the north.

After this was another gap in deliveries until the next two arrived at the end of 1986. They replaced F-27s on the **SAS** route between Luleå and Kiruna.

The tenth and last 340 arrived in August 1987, and was put into service on Swedair's 'own' route from Örebro to Copenhagen (replacing a Jetstream 31). Thus, Swedair had received all ten 340s it had ordered. However, regional services were successful and more 340s were needed. Consequently, Swedair ordered more aircraft, two in 1988 and one in 1989 to make a fleet of 13 Saab 340s.

The success of the 340s can have a flipside as Swedair soon found out. Traffic on the Borlänge increased by 72 per cent in the first three years of 340 operations and consequently Swedair replaced the 340 with Fokker F-28s from January 1988. It was partially compensated by introducing 340s on the Västerås–Copenhagen route on behalf of SAS from March 1988.

The year 1988 saw other major changes at Swedair. The target towing business, the general aviation representations and maintenance was sold out to FFV, and Swedair decided to concentrate on regional airline business only. In the same year Karl-Erik Strand left to go to the Swedish State Railway company. Swedair also had an air-taxi company called Basair which was sold to Nordflyg. Apart from the airline business Swedair kept the contracts for managing various regional airports such as Gällivare, Gävle, Västerås and Skövde. More changes followed in 1989 when Linjeflyg took over the 50 per cent shareholding held by the Swedish government, thus making it a majority shareholder with 75 per cent. The remaining 25 per cent is owned by ABA. In January 1989 Swedair also inaugurated a new route, Trollhättan–Copenhagen (the route was later discontinued). This was followed by Skövde–Stockholm in August the same year. In 1990 Swedair negotiated a possible

merger with Salair but these discussions were discontinued early 1991. Once these negotiations were broken off, Swedair went ahead and ordered three Saab 2000 for delivery 1993-94. By now ABA had purchased Linjeflyg's 75 per cent share and now completely controls Swedair. In 1989 Swedair carried 70,000 passengers on its SAS routes, 499,000 on its Linjeflyg routes and 27,000 on its own routes, making 596,000 in total. Its current general manager is Carsten Lundahl and it has 600 employees. Headquarters are at Arlanda Airport outside Stockholm.

Saab 340A Fleet

SE-ISO	013	Dec.84/	
SE-ISP	015	Jan.85/	
SE-ISR	017	Jan.85/	
SE-ISS	033	Sep.85/	
SE-IST	035	Oct.85/	
SE-ISU	042	Dec.85/	
SE-ISV	045	Jan.86/	Leased to Express Apr.90
SE-ISX	067	Oct.86/	
SE-ISY	080	Dec.86/	Leased to Express Dec.89
SE-ISZ	097	Aug.87/	
SE-ISN	137	Dec.88/	
SE-ISD	145	Apr.89/	
SE-ISE	156	Aug.89/	
LN-NVD	037	Dec.85/Feb.86	Leased from Norving
SE-ISC	008	Feb.86/Mar86	Leased from Saab
		Aug.86/Oct.86	Leased from Saab
SE-E69	069	Nov.86/Dec.86	Leased from Saab
LN-NVF	087	Feb.88/Apr.88	Leased from JB Aviation
HB-AHR	126	May 90/Jun.90	Leased from Crossair

Previous page, one of Swedair's 340As at its home-base, Stockholm (Arlanda) *(Author)*
Swedair has just launched a new livery as shown above *(T. Lakmaker)*

SWEDISH AIR FORCE

Sweden

The Swedish Air Force was set up as an independent force in 1926. Since the early days one of its tasks has been the transportation of 'VIPs' including both high ranking military officers as well as representatives of the government and Royal family. In the late 1930s the equipment was a DH.90 Dragonfly. During the 1940s it was a Beech 18. Then came again another de Havilland aircraft namely the DH.104 Dove which remained in service until 1966. In the early 1970s two Pembrokes were converted for the VIP role and specially painted. The early 1980s saw some leased Cessna 404s assuming the role, soon to be replaced by a Swearingen Metro in 1984. This aircraft reaffirmed the need for a dedicated VIP aircraft but the size of the aircraft was somewhat limiting and its 'customers' soon requested something more comfortable. For the Air Force the choice was obvious but the funding not so obvious! However, in February 1989 the government gave the Material Purchase Department the authorization to order one 340B with an executive interior. The specially equipped 340 was officially handed over on February 23, 1990. Interior arrangement is made for 17 passengers, divided in two departments, each with its own lavatory. It is based at the downtown Bromma Airport in Stockholm and is flown by pilots from the F-16 wing in Uppsala. Stewardesses are borrowed from Linjeflyg. On March 3, the Swedish King and Queen used the aircraft for the first time when they flew to Jönköping on an official visit.

Saab 340B ('Tp100')
'100001'   170   Feb.90/

Swedish Air Force's smartly painted 340B *(Saab/N-G. Widh)*

TAN (TX)

Argentina

TAN, or Transportes Aereos Neuquen, was founded by the local province of Neuquen in 1972. The aim was to establish a local air service within the province of Neuquen and neighbouring provinces which were not served by trunk airlines.

Initial equipment was four Piper Navajos purchased from the Argentine Army. Two of these were traded in as part payment for three brand new Rockwell 690s in 1977 and then followed two Metro IIIs purchased directly from Fairchild in 1980. As traffic grew during the early 1980s, TAN started evaluating pressurised 30 seat aircraft. It selected the Saab 340, and ordered one aircraft in June 1987. This was delivered in September the same year and entered service on November 4 on the Bahia Blanca route.

TAN had by now consolidated itself as the regional airline of southern Argentina and from its base at Neuquen flies to Mendoza, Malargue, Chos Malal in the north, and San Martin, Bariloche, Esquel, Comodoro Rivadavia and Trelew in the south, as well as Puerto Montt in Chile. It carries about 35,000 passengers per year and has 75 employees. For the last few years TAN has been headed by Tulio Ferraresso and Eduardo Rosa. In 1988 it started co-operating with Austral and they currently link their schedules together. As the military airline LADE, which is cleared to carry civilian passengers, has been reducing its network in the last few years, TAN hopes to fill the void and contine its gradual expansion. The Saab 340 mainly flies the four weekly services to Mendoza via Chos Malal and Malargue, the three weekly service to Comodoro Rivadavia via Bariloche and Esquel, as well as the twice weekly service to Puerto Montt.

Saab 340A Fleet

LV-AXV   094   Sep.87/

TAN's single 340A overflying the Andees *(Saab/N. Pealing)*

TATRA AIR (QS)   Czechoslovakia

Recent changes in Eastern Europe have rapidly changed the operating environment for many airlines. For some it has been the death-knell and they have vanished, for example Interflug. For others, it has meant an opportunity to buy or lease Western made aircraft, and most national carriers have by now done so. In some cases it has created new business opportunities serving needs which are not met by the national carriers.

Tatra Air is such an example. In July 1990, Slov Air signed an agreement with Crossair to set up a new regional airline in Bratislava. Slov Air provided two thirds of the capital, and **Crossair** the rest. Total start-up capital is $1.2 million. Crossair also provided the first aircraft, a Saab 340A, as well as all training of the staff and all maintenance.

The first 340 arrived in April 1991, and entered service on the Bratislava–Zurich routes twice a day, morning and evening. At midday it flies to Munich.

Current plans call for a second 340 in the autumn of 1991. With this aircraft, Tatra Air intends to expand its network to more destinations in Germany, as well as new destinations in Austria and northern Italy. Later on, Tatra Air may fly to Poland and Yugoslavia.

Saab 340A Fleet

OK-RGS	020	Apr.91/	Leased from LX
OK-	—	Autumn 91 planned	

Tatra's single 340A in its new smart livery *(A. Härry)*

TEMPELHOF AIRWAYS (CL)   Germany/USA

Tempelhof Airways USA Inc (TAUSA), as its full name reads, was founded in Fort Lauderdale, Florida in 1981, by Captain Knut Kramer, its current President. Its first aircraft was a Piper Navajo, and with this aircraft it began an air-taxi service from Berlin to Kassel. As the name indicates, the airline was based at Tempelhof Airport in Berlin, but flew under US registration due to the previous allied status of Berlin. Less than a year later, a Cessna Conquest was added to provide ambulance and air rescue service. In January 1985, the same aircraft began flying between Berlin and Paderborn for Nixdorf Computer AG. Initially these flights were charters but on September 29 of the same year, the carrier received its licence to operate scheduled service on this route using a Nord 262.

In July 1986, it began operating a Learjet 25D on behalf of the German Air Rescue Service. Three months later, it began flying the Berlin–Dortmund route using a second Nord 262. During 1987, Tempelhof carried over 40,000 passengers and as traffic was increasing, a decision was taken to start replacing the N-262s with Saab 340s. The first 340 was purchased directly from the manufacturer and delivered on July 12 1988, and placed into service on August 7. At the same time, Tempelhof was negotiating with Air Midwest regarding the possible purchase of three 340As, however these talks were discontinued during spring 1989. Instead Tempelhof leased another 340A from JB Aviation in June 1989. Tempelhof also had unsuccessful talks with TWA to operate the Berlin–Brussels route on their behalf but with the delivery of the second 340, a new daily route was opened to Luxembourg. A third 340 was purchased from Saab in August 1989, and four months later a new route was opened to Hamburg. At the same time, Tempelhof Airways became an IATA member. 1989 saw an increase of total passengers to 51,000.

The start of 1990 saw Tempelhof evaluating routes to Brussels and Milan, while at the same time negotiating with LAPA in Argentina for the possible lease of another 340. LAPA's President Andrew Deutsch became a shareholder in Tempelhof.

By this time the dramatic events in East Germany were rapidly changing the business environment of the airline, and consequently all expansion plans were put on a hold. The DHC-7 was briefly evaluated as the 340s were recording loadfactors of 70 per cent on the Dortmund and Hamburg routes, but once again no deal was concluded.

Up to now Tempelhof had remained a US airline operating aircraft on the US register. With the unification of Germany, Tempelhof needed to get restructured as a German airline, but this required further investment. As the current owners decided against this, Tempelhof took the drastic decision to drop all scheduled services in October 1990. Instead it leased out its 340s to RFG and Sabena, and decided to concentrate on handling all new regional airline services coming into Berlin (Tempelhof) Airport.

RFG took over the services to Dortmund and Paderborn using two Tempelhof 340s, while Sabena began the Brussels–Berlin service using the remaining 340. The Hamburg route was dropped.

Saab 340A Fleet

N109TA	121	Jul.88/Oct.90	'My Fair Lady'
N110TA	087	Jun.89/Oct.90	'Cabaret'. Leased from JB Aviation
N120TA	151	Aug.89/Oct.90	'Ein, Zwei, Drei'

A pre-delivery shot of Tempelhof's first 340 *(Saab/J. Lindahl)*

Crossair's contribution to Switzerland's 700th birthday was this Saab 340 especially painted in a livery designed by eight year old Giacomo Fiscalini and unveiled on January 23 1991. *(Crossair)*